Charles W Le Gendre

How to Deal with China

A Letter to De B. Rand. Keim, Esquire, Agent of the United States

Charles W Le Gendre

How to Deal with China
A Letter to De B. Rand. Keim, Esquire, Agent of the United States

ISBN/EAN: 9783337048785

Printed in Europe, USA, Canada, Australia, Japan

Cover: Foto ©ninafisch / pixelio.de

More available books at **www.hansebooks.com**

HOW TO DEAL WITH CHINA.

A LETTER TO DE B. RAND. KEIM, ESQUIRE,

AGENT OF THE UNITED STATES.

BY

GENERAL CHAS. W. LE GENDRE,

U. S. CONSUL AT AMOY.

AMOY

Printed by ROZARIO, MARCAL & CO.

MDCCCLXXI.

HOW TO DEAL WITH CHINA.

HOW TO DEAL
WITH CHINA.

A LETTER TO DE B. RAND. KEIM, ESQUIRE,

AGENT OF THE UNITED STATES.

BY

GENERAL CHAS. W. LE GENDRE,

U. S. CONSUL AT AMOY.

AMOY
Printed by ROZARIO, MARCAL & CO.

MDCCCLXXI.

The manuscript from which this paper was printed was written in great haste and not as legibly as it might have been, and it was passed through the press by, and under the supervision of Macao-Portugese and Chinese, persons comparatively ignorant of the English language; the consequence is that so many errors have crept into the text that the author has abandoned the task of drawing up a table of errata, as hopeless.

ROMYN HITCHCOCK.

U. S. Consulate for Amoy and the Dependencies thereof.

AMOY, 5th June, 1871.

To the Hon. First Assistant Secretary of State
WASHINGTON, D. C.

SIR,

I have the honor to transmit, through you, a paper which I have prepared for Mr. Keim, who came to inspect my consulate, in January last.

In undertaking this task I have been guided by two conderations: First, to give to the Country the benefit of the experience which I have acquired, in its service, during a residence of five years in the East; and, in the second place, to be of use to an officer specially recommended by the President, in assisting him in making his report to the Government more fully than he otherwise could have done with the unavoidably imperfect information that he was enabled to gather during his brief stay in China.

In the preparation of this paper I have availed myself of the experience which I have acquired during my repeated and protracted visits to Formosa. This Island represents China in miniature, with many of its varieties of race, each speaking different dialects, with all its literary aspects, its administrative and military organization, its

(II)

wonderful agriculture and commerce, all of which the observer may embrace within a narrow space, under the Imperial Rule, not exceeding two hundred miles in length by twenty in breadth. There I have studied the inland trade in its connection with the collection of public revenue under a system peculiar to the Chinese, in its complex forms and features; and in an uninterrupted intercourse with the authorities and people there, I have been enabled to obtain an insight into subjects which would have otherwise been closed to me; and with what personal observation had not furnished me, I have obtained in communications with men who had past the best years of their lives in public employ in this country, and by whose experience it has been my good fortune to profit.

I have had only one hundred copies of this paper printed, twenty [forty struck through] of which I now beg to hand you for circulation as you may think fit. I have kept the remainder in the Consular Archives, save three copies which I have sent, to the Consul General, to the Minister and the Admiral. I shall wait the Department's permission before presenting any of them to my friends.

I have the honor to be,

Sir,

Your obedient Servant,

CHAS. W. LE GENDRE.

CONTENTS.

	PAGE.
A letter to the first Assistant Secretary of State	
A letter to Mr. Keim, Agent of the United States	1
I. The Literati and their influence in the Government of China	7
II. The Twenty-first of June, and the Diplomacy in Peking	33
III. A Trip overland from Foochow to Amoy	53
IV. The Disturbances in the Amoy District, previous to the Massacres of Tientsin, and how they were dealt with	69
V. A plan for the better transaction of foreign affairs in the interior of the Empire between the Consuls and the Chinese	93
VI. Conclusions	125
Appendix	135

United States Consulate for Amoy and the dependencies thereof

Amoy, 25th April, 1871.

DE B. RAND. KEIM, Esquire,

Agent of the United States,

Washington, D. C.

SIR:

You ask me to give you a series of memorandums upon various questions of interest to us, and which I had opportunities to study during my term of five years, in China. While, in touching subjects which have been treated by men of great weight, I have somewhat hesitated in offering my views, I have conceived myself entitled to write fully on others a knowledge of which the unusually favorable position I had been placed in had afforded me facilities to acquire which others had not possessed.

Doubtless you have read a great deal upon the disturbances which have occurred in China during the last two years and you have heard much concerning the last massacre at Tient-sien; but, unless you look for an explanation of this lamentable trajedy in records not generally open to daily investigation, I doubt whether you will see in it anything but what most of the people have, that is to say, a street disturbance which hardly deserves notice, unless it is taken as exhibiting a state of barbarism of the Chinese nation for which previous accounts had not prepared us. It is those records which I have endeavoured to throw open before you, in a concise form, in memorandums first and second. The first may be called the philosophy of the 21st of June and of the scenes of violence which have preceded it at other points in the Empire, and which may yet prove to be but the prelude of more revolting transactions. The second is simply the history of the massacre of Tient-sien, and of the manner it was dealt with by the Chargé d'Affaires for France, as given to me by a gentleman whom you have advantageously known during your visit in the East, and who has been, as you are aware of, intimately connected with the negociations that took place both in Tient-sien and Peking, after the occurrence, between Count Rochechouart and the Tsung-lee-yamûn.

The plea that has been put forward to serve as an excuse for the "Laisser faire" policy pursued, of late years, with the Chinese, that the Imperial Government lacks the power to control the provincial Governors and the latter, through the minor authorities, the populace in the interior of the Empire, is, in my opinion, to be accepted, to say the least, with extreme reserve. I believe that, upon further enquiry, it will be found that, so long as the people are not incited against foreigners, they are most hospitable; and whenever the agents of the Emperor, in the Provinces, are guided by the maxims of profound wisdom which they profess to respect and which are laid down in their books of moral philosophy, all under them are docile and submissive. With a view to practically demonstrate this to you, I have brought you from Foochow to Amoy, overland, and now I offer you the relation of our trip, as written by a servant of the Chinese, that it may remain as a standing evidence of our joint experience. This will be memorandum No. 3.

Memorandum No. 4 is interesting as showing the means by which in 1869, my lamented colleague and friend, Mr. Gibson, British Consul a, Taiwanfoo, Island of Formosa, compelled the authorities to make use of the power they have over their people, in punishing them for acts of violence they had committed against foreign residents, and to which, he had good motives to believe, the local officers had incited them. This paper will exhibit more fully the advantages of a system of reprisals as inaugurated by Mr. Gibson, when I say that, after his administration of one year, the whole province of Fohkien had enjoyed a state of order and peace for which the experience of former years had not justified one to look for.

"As it is the Empire is no longer ruled; its provinces are held together solely by the force of cohesion and the desire of the people for peace and of their love for order and quiet. The state is drifting to and fro, and the sole concern of many of those in power is to hold their places. As long as this state of affairs will last, any attempt to repress the rebellions simply by the sword will be found ineffectual. Crushed in one place, they will spring up, like a weed, in another; because the causes of the rebellions are not to be found in the people, but in that nest of corruption at Peking. To put down rebellions, the augean stables, first, must be cleansed."(1) But how shall this be done? An answer to this question. I have endeavoured to give in memoraudum No 5. "A plan for the better transtaction of foreign affairs in the interior of the Empire by the Chinese," and in the concluding remarks of this paper.

You will be surprised that I submit no suggestions for the better protection of missionaries both foreign and native. I do not undervalue missionary enterprise, but I firmly believe that our greatest concern should be to afford an efficient protection to our trade in the interior of the Empire, not only as a sacred obligation contracted by the country with such of our citizens who have invested their means in the China trade under the faith of the existing treaties, but also as the most sure and practical means of advancing civilization in the East, and in view of this, a most desirable end, rather than Christianity should take the lead and that Commerce should move on the path traced by the apostles of our faith, I advise that Christianity should follow on the road open by Trade.

I have the honor to be,.

Sir,

Yours respectfully

CHS. W. LE GENDRE.

---

(1) Our interests in China. by Horatio N. Lay, C. B., late Inspector General of Chinese Customs at Peking, London, 1864.

MEMORANDUM No. 1.

THE LITERATI AND THEIR INFLUENCE
IN THE GOVERNMENT OF CHINA.

(7)

Memorandum No. 1.

THE LITERATI,
AND THEIR INFLUENCE IN THE GOVERNMENT IN CHINA.

> "Avec le monde a commencé une guerre qui doit finir avec le monde, et pas avant, celle de l'homme contre la nature, de l'esprit contre la matière, de la Liberté contre la fatalité. L'histoire n'est pas autre chose que le recit de cette lutte." (J. Michelet. Introduction à l'histoire universalle, page 1).

The late massacres at Tientsin offer but a new instance of the madness of man when blinded by fanaticism and priestcraft.

Before the new era, inaugurated by Luther and Calvin, had fairly commenced in Europe, Germany and Switzerland had their stakes, (1404-1553), France, Italy and Spain, their Inquisition (1478), their St. Bartholomew (1572), the revocation of the Edict of Nantes (1685); and now it is China's turn, on the eve, let us hope, of a great transformation, to give us the sad spectacle of her mournful hecatombs. This will become apparent by a reference to the religious principles of the ruling classes in that great Empire.

Revelation according to Y-king.
Confucius writes: "Ty-kih is revealed in Y-king. (1) "What does Ty-kih mean? It means the Chaos, when light and darkness were not; the one not having been separated from the other. There is no name for Ty-kih; therefore it was called Ty-kih. From Ty-kih comes Liang-e (divine object, the creation), which itself is formed of Ty-yang (eternity, male, man, sun, light &c.) and Ty-ying (moon, night, female, everything which is uncertain), (2) *(Y-king, book 5th. page 14 (3),).* Ty-kih, Liang-e, Ty-yang

---
(1) *Ty*, in Chinese, means, the utmost point, greatest &c.; and *Kih*, extreme.
(2) *Liang-e*, comes from *Liang*, two, and, *E*, power of nature — *Yang*, in *Ty-yang*, signifies, sun, or the superior of two things in contact; while *Yn*, in *Ty-yin*, means, moon, or the inferior of two things in contact.
(3) The following is the Chinese text of this quotation of Y-King.

易經
繫辭卷五
十四篇

是故易有太極
是生兩儀
兩儀生四象
四象生八卦
八卦定吉凶
吉凶生大業

and *Ty-ying*, are the abstract ideas upon which the system of thoughts of the Chinese, so to speak, is based; and the radicals of their system of writing are their corresponding symbols.

These Symbols are for *Ty-kih*, a circle, ◯ , for *Liang-e*, a circle divided in two parts, one black and the other white, with a dot on the right corner, representing the moon rising in the heavens, ☯ . The upper part of the latter figure represents *Ty-yang*, and the lower one *Ty-ying*.

The first radical is made of the circumference of the circle unrolled; it is a single and continuous line, thus, ——— and it conveys the idea of Heaven, of light, of what is eternal, infinite, innumerable, invariable, affirmed, &c. The same line broken, interrupted; thus, —— ——, makes the second radical, which represents darkness, finite things, earth, time, contradiction, &c. &c.

Now from the combination of both lines, as from the combination of the heavens and the earth, of darkness and of light, all the other signs are derived, of which the most prominent are those that designate the waters without limits, ☵, the winds, ☴, ether, fire, ☲ the the mountains, ☶, thunder, ☳ &c. In this manner, the heavens and the earth, the infinite and the finite, represented by strokes, are the A, B, C of the Chinese written language. According to tradition it was given to man by Foh-he, who himself received it from God.

The Chinese revealer Foh-he 伏羲, (1) was born from a virgin who conceived him while walking solitarily on the foot-steps of an old man. "Foh-he's, mother was living near a small river, at a place called *Hwa-su*, 華胥, situated in the hien (district) called *Lan Ti-en*, 藍田縣 in the province of *Shen-si*," 陝西 (2). She saw the ghost of a man passing by, and she walked on his foot steps; she felt a sensation in her breast;

---

(1) *Foh-he*, 伏羲, is also named *Pou-he*, 包羲. The Chinese *Foh*, 伏, means, *inclosed* in (the *Empire*) and *he*, *Supreme ruler*: The *Supreme ruler of the Empire* — Confucius says in his commentary of Y-King. —" *Foh-he*, had every thing *within himself*." Y-King commentary by Confucius, book 5, page 18.

(2) The region west of the yellow river.

a rainbow, as a halo of glory, encircled her head; she was pregnant; and Foh-he was born from her in the district of Ching-ki, 成紀. The two principles were concentrated in Foh-he, and he had within himself the goodness of all creation (1).

Foh-he went to the low lands, on the banks of the Wha-seu river; there he found, attached to the slime, a monstrous animal. Some say a turtle, some say a dragon horse (2) on whose scales, of the color of the heavens, were mysterious figures written, bearing the stamp of eternal wisdom. The Hantou (river picture) 河圖 was revealed to him from the waters (3).

(1) Being so born (of heaven) like winds (that spread and move rapidly) he had the beneficient influence of the holy spirit and the brightness of the sun and of the moon— therefore he became the first ruler (of China).—*Kang-kien-pu*, literally signifies, *Kang*, 綱 great principles, *Kien*, 鑑, *mirror*, and *Pu*, 補, *supplement*. The two last characters Kien, 鑑, and Pu, 補, taken together, mean history.

(2) Although the Turtle is not referred to in the Y-King commentary by Confucius, there is no doubt that it was known before his time. (Y-King-ty-tche, 1st Book, 2nd page.)

(3) The Dragon—Horse emerged from the waters, and, according to tradition, he had in him the spirit of Heaven and of Earth. He resembled a horse with the scales of a Dragon and therefore, he was called a Dragon-Horse. He was 8 feet 5 inches in height, of about the size of a camel. He had wings so that he could move on the water, without danger. He came in those days, there being a wise man (Foh-e) capable to understand his teachings (Kang-kien-pu—8th page, 1st Book.)

To those figures (1) Foh-he compared the general features of the universe; the great strokes formed in the heavens, from the lines of the stars; on the earth, from the winding of the streams and the uneveness of mounts; and, from all this, he conceived the rudiments of writing.

Foh-he looked at the heavens and, below, he saw the earth. Then he made the Pah-kwa, or the eight principles or sources (2). The Pah-kwa is to man the source of all inspiration, the recipient of all knowledge (3).

This gigantic conception of writing formed in the image of the creation, this miracle of an art which is akin to magic, is what has infatuated the Chinese the most, and to a point that they have neglected everything else, as, very properly, remarked to me by admiral Litchenn Miou, of Amoy. In one word, God who is revealed to the Indians by the light, to the Greeks by the lyre, is disclosed to the Chinese by the prodigy of writing.

(1) Therefore he came and looked at the heavens, at the earth and at the ten thousand things which existed between the heavens and the earth and to all these he compared the Pah-kwa. (Kang-kien-pu, 8th page, 1st book.)

綱鑑補 卷一 八篇

於是仰觀象於天俯觀法於地中觀萬物於人始畫八卦

(2) Foh-e looked at the heavens and below, he saw the earth, and he caused men and women to live as husband and wife; afterwards he divided every thing into five classes: water, fire, wood, metal, (or gold) and earth. He made the natural laws for man's guidance; he found the Pah-kwa or the eight principles or sources. He was the first to unite the people under one rule; and all were content. So they called him Foh-e. (—Kang-kien-pu, Book 1st, page 7.)

綱鑑補 第七篇 卷一

伏羲仰觀象如天俯察法如地因夫婦正五行始定人道畫八卦以定天下伏而化之故謂之伏羲也

(3) In the Pah-kwa, all that is known and all that is unknown may be looked for. It comprises good omens and bad omens; in it lie the records of the past and the secrets of the future. It is the source of all knowledge. (Y-King, commentory by confucious—Book V. page 14.)

繫辭 卷五 十四篇

八卦定吉凶吉凶生大業

(11)

Traced under the eyes of the Master, those wonderful characters are the types of an infinity of relations, of true principles, discovered

THE PAH-KWA. According to Foh-c (Y-King Ti-chu, Book I, 3rd page.)   (Fig. 1.)
SOUTH.

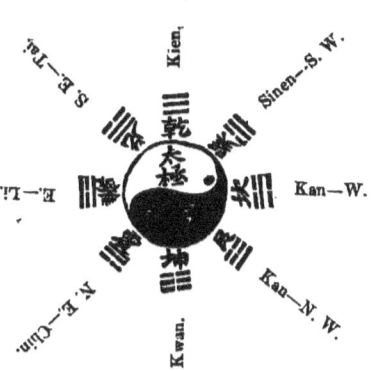

Tai, Earth (Land & water) &c.
Li, Sun, &c.
Chin, Thunder, animal & vegetable life &c.&c.
Kwan, the Earth, inferior or obsequious to Heaven, hence applied to the moon, to wife, &c.

Kien, Heaven, the power of, agency of Heaven, Father, Mother. Emperor, Minister &c.   1. Earth; 2, Man; 3. Heaven.
Sinen, wind, mildness, &c.
Kan, water &c.
Kan, mountain, &c.

NORTH.
Hautau, or the figures as seen on the back of the Dragon-Horse, according to Y-King Chiu-i Ting-kee, Book II. page 53.   (Fig. 2.)

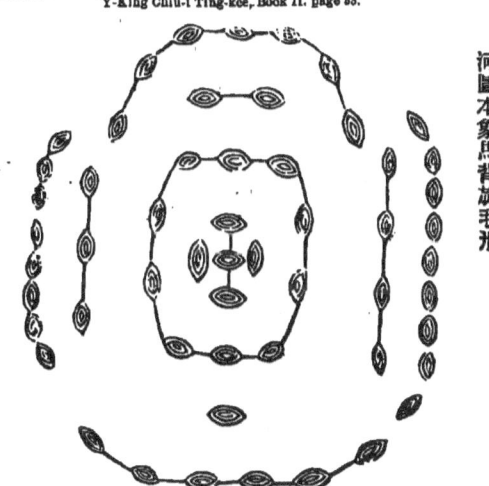

(12)

through investigation and meditation. For this revelation must inces-

洛書本象龜甲坼文形
Lah-Sheu, or the figures seen on the Turtoise shells, according to Y-King, Chiu-i Ting-kea. Book II. page 53. (Fig. 3.)

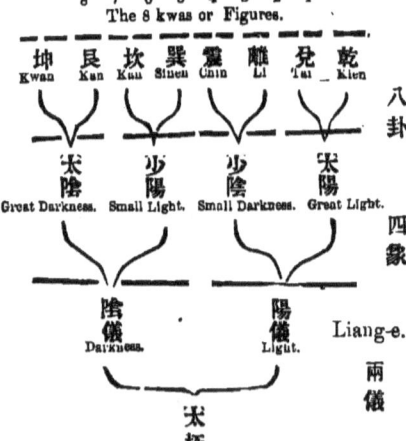

Foh-e's first conception of the Pah-kwa, Chiu-i Ting-ku Book II. page 52. (Y-king.) (Fig. 4.)

santly remain present to the thoughts of the wise and be their text. Each character is a symbol, a proverb that shows forth its deepest sig-

The diagram of the record from the Lo River, with the nine classifications as given in the book of Show. Section VI of the Shoo-king.

(Fig. 5.)

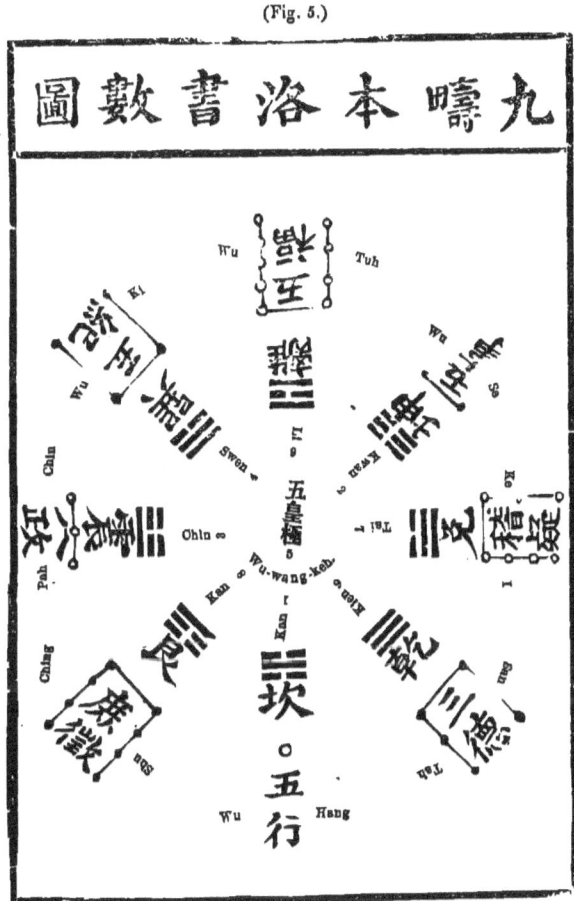

nification to those that study it with religious care; and those types,

In connection with the diagrams, it is said that Heaven conferred on Yu (B. C. 1,121) the divine turtoise, bearing a book out of the river; on its back were various numbers up to 9. Yu arranged them, and completed the nine species. The Y-king says that the Yellow river produced the delination of the Hautou, and the Lo river the treatise or the characters as given in the Pah-kwa. As Section VI of the book of show is rather short and yet gives a complete commentary of the diagram from the record of the Lo river, I copy here the excellent translation which the late Mr. W. H. Medhurst, sen. has made of it.

SECTION VI. *The great plan.*—On the 13th year (B. C. 1, 121,) the king went to enquire of Kê-tszè; When the king seriously addressed him, saying, Oh you Kê-tszè! Heaven has secretly settled the lower people, aiding and according with that in which they rest: but I do not know the arrangement of those invariable principles.

Kê-tszè as seriously replied, saying, I have heard that, in old time, Kwän tried to stop the overwhelming waters, and improperly interfered with the five elements; the Supreme Ruler was moved with indgination, and withheld from him the great plan, with the nine classifications: thus the invariable principles were destroyed, and Kwän was driven to death. Yü then rose as his successor, and Heaven gave to Yü the great plan and the nine classifications, so that the invariable principles were arranged.

The first of these was, the five elements; the second in order was, a respectful use of the five senses; the third was, an economical attention to the eight regulations; the fourth was, a harmonious use of the five arrangers; the fifth was, an established performance of the princely perfections; the sixth was, a well-regulated carrying out of the three virtues; the seventh was, an intelligent attention to the examination of doubts; the eighth was, a considerate use of the general verifications; the ninth was, an earnest tending towards the five blessings, and an awe-struck avoiding of the six extreme visitations.

In the first place, there were the five elements; the first (of which) was called water, the second was fire, the third was wood, the fourth was metal, and the fifth was earth. Water is described as dripping down, and fire as blazing up; wood is sometimes crooked and sometimes straight; metal is now yielding and then hard; while (the properties of) earth are displayed in sowing and reaping. That which drips down becomes brackish (as the sea,) that which blazes up becomes bitter (as soot,) that which is occasionally crooked and straight becomes sour, (as certain vegetables,) that which is at times yielding and hard becomes acid, (as the taste of some metals,) and that which is sown and reaped becomes sweet (as corn). (For the Symbol, see No. 1, Fig. 5).

In the second place, there were the five senses, the first of which was called shape, the second termed speech, the third denominated sight, the fourth was called hearing, and the fifth was entitled thinking. * Shape may be referred to respect, speech may be classed under compliance, sight may be ranked with clearness, hearing may be arranged under perception, and thought allied to intelligence. Respect produces veneration, compliance is the foundation of government, clearness leads to knowledge, perception to device, and intelligence to perfect wisdom. (For the Symbol, see No. 2, Fig. 5).

In the third place, there were the eight regulators; the first of which was called the provider of food, the second was termed the gatherer of property, † the third was denominated the presenter of offerings, the fourth was entitled the superintendent of public works, the fifth was called the minister of instruction, the sixth was considered as the criminal judge, the seventh was made (the receiver) of guests, and the eight was promoted to be general of the army. (For the Symbol, see No. 3, Fig. 5).

---

* *When men are first born their external form is completed, after coming into the world, their voice is heard; after awhile they can see; subsequent to this they hear; and in the course of time they begin to think.*

† *Food is that which people have most urgent need of, property is that on which men mainly depend, hence they are put in the first and second place.*

taken together, form the representation of all the facts, in the physical

In the fourth place, there were the five arrangers; the first of which was called the circuit of the seasons, the second was called the moon, the third was denominated the sun, the fourth was termed the stars, and the fifth was referred to the astronomical calculations. (For the Symbol, see No. 4, Fig. 5).

In the fifth place, there were the princely perfections. Let the prince establish the point of perfection, and accumulating the five kinds of blessings, let him diffusively confer them on the common people; then the common people, on account of his perfections, will afford him perfect protection. ‡ (For the Symbol, see No. 5, Fig. 5).

Whenever the common people avoid cabals, and the officers keep from forming factions, it is solely because the prince has attained perfection.

When there are any among the common people who display contrivance, activity, and determination, let your Majesty bear them in mind. When any are not yet joined to perfect goodness, and still not invigled in crime, * let the prince then take them in hand; while on those who wear a placid countenance, and profess to be enamoured with virtue, do you then confer emolument. Thus these people will attain to the perfection of the prince.

Do not oppress the poor and solitary, nor dread the high and honourable. †

When officers display capacity and activity, promote their views, and the country will be prosperous. All the magistrates being well paid, insist on their doing good; if you cannot render them comfortable in their own families, these men will soon be involved in crimes; ‡ and when they are averse to virtue, although you confer on them emolument, you will only render yourself an accomplice in their villainies.

In order to prevent partiality and injustice, let (the people) follow the royal rectitude; in order to avoid excessive attachments, let them obey the royal doctrines; in order to exclude extreme antipathies, let them pursue the royal way. When they are without partialities and cabals, the royal doctrines will be enlarged and extended; when party spirit and prejudices cease, the royal way will be easy and unobstructed; when there are no rebellions nor corruptions, the royal course will be straight and even; (thus the people) will be brought together to perfection, and will revert to extreme goodness.

He proceeded to observe, that the wide-spread inculcation of the princely perfections, is none other than the invariable principle, and the right kind of instruction; it is also the instruction sanctioned by the Supreme.

....

‡ *This means that the prince ought to carry out to the utmost the duties of the human relations. Thus in regard to the relation subsisting between parents and children he should be extremely affectionate, and then all the parents and children would take him for a pattern. Thus also with regard to the conjugal and fraternal relations, let the prince first set a perfect pattern, and the whole empire will imitate him. In this way the suitability of rational principles being invariably carried out in every word and action, without a hair's breadth of excess or defect, the point of perfection will be established. Now perfection is the foundation of happiness, and happiness is the certain result of perfection; wherever perfection is established happiness will certainly accumulate. But the prince does not accumulate happiness merely to benefit his own person; he aims likewise to disseminate that happiness abroad among the people, so that every one may be affected and transformed by his example; this is what is called diffusing blessings abroad among the people. The people seeing this will defend their prince to the utmost, and not dare to desert him.*

* *These are men of mediocrity; if encouraged, they will practise virtue, but if neglected, they will sink into vice; hence the prince should take them in hand.*

† *This means, that should the meanest of the people practise virtue, they ought to be encouraged; and if the great and noble do wrong, they must be reproved.*

‡ *When salaries are not regularly paid, and the necessaries of life not afforded, then men cannot be comfortable at home, and will soon take improper means to supply their wants.*

and spiritual order, the knowledge of which is required for one's guid-

Whenever the common people carry out these wide-spread instructions, they teach them and practise them, in order to approximate to the splendour of the Son of Heaven; while they say, the Emperor is the people's parent, and thus he becomes the ruler of all sublunary things.

In the sixth place, there are the three virtues, the first of which is called evenhanded justice, the second is denominated strict rule, and the third is termed a mild course of government. In peaceful and tranquil times, be strictly just. When the people are obstinate and unyielding, rule them by severity; when they are harmonious and compliant, govern them with mildness; when they are deeply sunk in barbarity, rule them with rigour; and when they are elevated in the scale of civilization, let your administration be lenient.

Only the sovereign should confer emoluments, and he only inflict punishments, while to the prince alone belongs the property of the state; the subject has nothing to do with conferring rewards, inflicting punishments, or administering the wealth of the nation.

When subjects confer emoluments, inflict punishments, or interfere with the disposal of the public property, then injury will accrue to their families, and ruin to their country. When men in office are corrupt, unjust, and selfish, the people will err and transgress. (For the Symbol, see No. 7, Fig. 5).

In the seventh place, there was the examination of doubts. (When doubts occur) select and appoint proper men to superintend the tortoise and reeds, and let them divine and prognosticate thereby.

(The divinations) are called, moisture, fair weather, obscurity, interrupted sucession, and mixture.

(The prognostics) are termed chastity, and penitence.

They are altogether seven, of which the divinations are five, and the prognostics two; (all of which are useful) in tracing out the errors of business.

Having appointed the proper officers to attend to divinations and prognostics, let three men carry on the auguries, and follow any two of them in their opinions.

Should you have any great doubts, appeal to your own judgment, and consult your nobles, as well as your people, while you attend at the same time to the divinations and prognostics. Should you assent, and the tortoise and reeds be favourable, your nobles and people all coinciding in the same views, this is what is called a grand concord; in such cases, your person will be secure, and your descendants will be happy. Should your own views be favourable to a project, and the tortoise and reeds assent, while the nobles and people object, it would be nevertheless favourable. Should your nobles, with the tortoise and reeds coincide, while you and the common people are averse to a measure, it may still be felicitous. When your people, the tortoise, and reeds all give a favourable answer, but you and your nobles scruple about an undertaking, you may yet consider it advantageous. Should you and the tortoise assent, while the reeds, the nobles, and the people demur, then internal operations might be felicitous, but external undertakings prejudicial. * But when the tortoise and reeds both oppose the views of man, to remain still would be advisable, and all active operations should be avoided. (For the Symbol, see No. 7, Fig. 5).

In the eighth place, there are the general verifications, namely, rain, fair weather, heat, cold, and wind; all which should accord with the proper seasons. When these five come fully prepared, each in its proper order, all kinds of vegetables will be exuberant.

When either of these are in excess, it is bad; when they were deficient, it is also bad.

There are the favourable verifications; for instance, respect is followed by reasonable showers; good government, by opportune fair weather; intelligence, by a due degree of heat; counsel, by a proper modicum of cold; and perfection, by periodical winds. The unfavourable verifications are these; dissoluteness, which is followed by incessant showers; error, by uninterrupted clear weather; indolence, by excessive heat; haste, by extreme cold; and stupidity, by perpetual tempests.

---
* *Internal operations refer to sacrificing, and external ones to war.*

A PLAN OF THE NINE-FOLD PATH OF THE MOON,
AS DRAWN BY THE CHINESE.

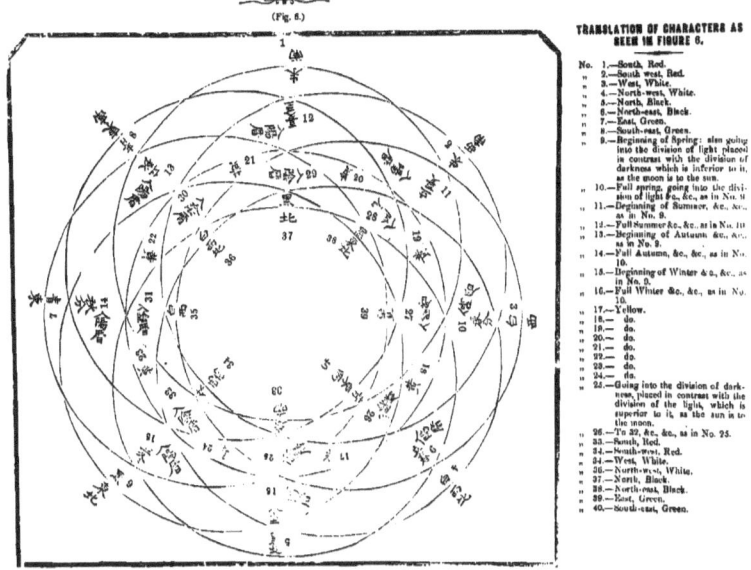

(Fig. 8.)

TRANSLATION OF CHARACTERS AS SEEN IN FIGURE 6.

No. 1.—South, Red.
 „ 2.—South-west, Red.
 „ 3.—West, White.
 „ 4.—North-west, White.
 „ 5.—North, Black.
 „ 6.—North-east, Black.
 „ 7.—East, Green.
 „ 8.—South-east, Green.
 „ 9.—Beginning of Spring; also going into the division of light placed in contrast with the division of darkness which is inferior to it, as the moon is to the sun.
 „ 10.—Full spring, going into the division of light &c., &c., as in No. 9.
 „ 11.—Beginning of Summer, &c., &c., as in No. 9.
 „ 12.—Full Summer &c. &c., as in No. 10.
 „ 13.—Beginning of Autumn &c., &c., as in No. 9.
 „ 14.—Full Autumn, &c., &c., as in No. 10.
 „ 15.—Beginning of Winter &c., &c., as in No. 9.
 „ 16.—Full Winter &c., &c., as in No. 10.
 „ 17.—Yellow.
 „ 18.— do.
 „ 19.— do.
 „ 20.— do.
 „ 21.— do.
 „ 22.— do.
 „ 23.— do.
 „ 24.— do.
 „ 25.—Going into the division of darkness, placed in contrast with the division of the light, which is superior to it, as the sun is to the moon.
 „ 26.—To 32, &c., &c., as in No. 25.
 „ 33.—South, Red.
 „ 34.—South-west, Red.
 „ 35.—West, White.
 „ 36.—North-west, White.
 „ 37.—North, Black.
 „ 38.—North-east, Black.
 „ 39.—East, Green.
 „ 40.—South-east, Green.

ance in life. "They are the science of that which is manifest and of

We should say, let the ruler examine himself with regard to the year, the nobles with respect to the month, † and the inferior magistrates with reference to the day.

When the years, months, and days, do not fail in their seasons, the various kinds of grain will ripen, government will be intelligent, clever people will be promoted, and families will be peaceful and settled.

When the days, months, and years, fail in their seasons, the various, kinds of grain will not come to perfection, government will be dark and devoid of intelligence, clever people will remain in obscurity, and families will not be tranquil.

The common people are like the stars; ‡ certain stars bring wind, while others produce rain; * the course of the sun and moon points out the winter and summer solstice, † and the moon's travelling among the fixed stars indicates the approach of wind and rain.

In the ninth place, there are the five kinds of happiness, one of which is called longevity, the second riches, the third tranquillity, the fourth the love of virtue, and the fifth a discovery of the proper termination of life. (For the symbol, See No. 9, Fig. 5).

The six extremities are; first an untimely and early death, secondly, sickness, thirdly, sorrow, fourthly, poverty, fifthly, hardihood in sin, and sixthly, indulgence in iniquity.

† *A king's success or failure in virtue would affect the year, a noble's the month, and an inferior officer's the day, each one according to his rank and station.*

‡ *That is the common people depend on their superiors, just like the stars are attached to the body of the heavens.*

* *The Constellation* 箕 *Kê (the hand of Sagittarius) brings wind, and the constellation* 畢 *Peih (Hyades) brings rian.*

† *The sun has a middle path, but the moon follows a nine-fold course; the middle path of the sun, is the ecliptic. On the north the moon in its course travels to the eastern part of* 井 *Tsing (the head of Gemini,) where it reaches its limit towards the (north) pole: on the south it goes to* 牛 *New (the head of Capricornus,) where it is furthest removed from the north pole; on the east it travels to the constellation* 角 *Kèo, (Spica Virginis:) and on the west to* 婁 *Leu, (the head of Aries,) both equi-distant from the poles. The nine courses of the moon are* 黑道 *the black path, on the north of the ecliptic, where it comes out twice;* 赤道 *the red path, (the equinoctial) on the south of the ecliptic, where it comes out twice;* 白道 *the white path to the west of the ecliptic, where it comes out twice;* 青道 *the azure path, to the east of the ecliptic, where it comes out twice; which, together with* 黃道 *the ecliptic itself, make nine courses. When the sun is at the extreme south,* 牽牛 *at the tropic of Capricorn, it forms the Winter Solstice; when at the extreme north,* 東井 *at the tropic of Cancer, it forms the Summer Solstice. Travelling between the south and north, easterly to* 角 *Virgo, and westerly to* 婁 *Aries, it forms the Vernal and Autumnal equinoxes. The moon, from the* 立春 *commencement of spring (See No. 9, figure 6) (February 5). to* 春分 *the Vernal Equinox, (See No. 10, figure 6) follows the azure path; from* 立秋 *the commencement of autumn, (See No. 13, figure 6) (Aug. 9.) to the* 秋分 *Autumnal Equinox, (See No. 14, figure 6) it follows the white path; from* 立冬 *the commencement of winter (See No. 15, figure 6) (Nov. 8.) to the* 冬至 *Winter Solstice, (See No. 16, figure 6) it follows the black path; and from the* 立夏 *commencement of summer (May 7.) to the* 夏至 *Summer Solstice, (See No. 11, figure 6) it follows the azure path equinotial.) Hence it is said, that the courses of the sun and moon produce winter, and summer. When the moon goes to the north-east, enters the constellation* 箕 *Kê,*

that which is not manifest; the source of all doctrine, of all writing, the origin of all knowledge." Confucius was fifty when he first understood the Pah-kwa; then only, also, so he tells us, he commenced to be wise. (1)

A certain character which is formed of the sign of Heaven and of that of water (the sea in motion) is the image of a courageous man who unmoved by the blows of fate, rests on the ruins of his home and affections. The conjunction of the two lines that figure the unison of earth and water, conveys the idea of sound politics based on that true friendship which should exist between two great Empires; but the space left between the line of the heavens and that of water or earth, ☰☵ is a hint to the legislator for a well understood distinction of classes, such as should be maintained in a well organized community (2). The sign of fire, placed at

(Sagittarius) there is much wind; when it travels to the south-west, and enters the constellation 畢 Peïh (Hyades) then there is much rain; hence it is said, that the moon in its journey among the stars produces wind and rain.

[*N. B. From the above representation of the sun's place at the four quarters of the year, it would appear, that the calculation must have been made when the equinoxes were 30 degrees distant from the point where they now are, or about 2000 years ago. The nine-fold course of the moon appears to refer to the inclination of the lunar orbit, and to the ascending and descending nodes, where they cut the ecliptic. A plan of the ninefold path of the moon, as drawn by the Chinese, will be found attached. (See fig. 6.).*

(1) (Sz-shû, 1st part, 4th Book, 5th page.) "My (Confucius) wish has been that I would live a few years after the age of fifty to study and understand Y-king and thus find myself fairly established on the road to wisdom." By this Confucius (this is a remark made by the commentator) meant that Y-king is a very deep book almost universal in its relations, that it must be studied with care. and that no one could expect to be able to master it after a rapid perusal.

(2) ☰ } Heaven.

☵ } Water, or Heaven above Water or the Earth,

is the character Lee and signifies foot standing on Earth. It is the symbol of the division of men into high and low classes. When one is walking, he finds that the heavens are above (his head), and the waters (or the earth) beneath; and this is a natural order of things which can not be changed. Hence the division of men (living in a state of society) in classes. (Chan-i-ting-kuo, 2nd Book, 4th page.)

四書上論卷四第五篇 周易訂詁二卷第二十四篇

子曰加我數年五十以學易可以無大過矣蓋

聖人深見易道之無窮

學易可以救人使知其

而言此以致人又不可

不可不學而

易而學也

而制其體履上者如天之不

可為澤下者如澤之不可為

志 天上下各得其分則民有定

the highest point in the heavens, expresses a law of nature and, at the same time, it is offered as a model to princes and men high in the scale of society, who should fill the whole universe with the splendor of their virtue (1). In one character, the delicate disposition of the stroke is the image of modesty (2). Indeed the discovery of all useful arts is owing to a protracted comtemplation of the sacred characters and constant efforts to imitate them. The secrets of weaving cloth, of stitching nets have their origin in the character Lee, ☰☰ (3).

(1) ☰☰ { 離 上 Fire above.

☰ { 乾 下 Heaven below, a fire high in the heavens (is a hint for a great minister) who has many duties to perform. Is there a disturbance, a revolt, it is his task to quell them. Whatever is too bitter, or too hot or even too sweet, be must make right. He has to clear up what is obscure or intricate; to give weight to that which is too light......A minister of state is like a big cart, it must be properly loaded before it can be put on the way....all his acts must be to the benefit of the King. (Chau-i-ting-koo, 2nd Book, page 55.)

(2) I give a few quotations of Y-king in which other Symbols are given for imitation by all men, as, in Catholic books, the cross is offered to believers as a source of inspiration.—"The mountains are in the Earth: it is the Kun (In imitation of it) learned, wise and good men search into all things that they may gradually improve. They are as correct as a scale, (and yet) they place themselves on a level with the shepherd;"— That is to say, mountains proceed from the earth where they had been lying hidden. In imitation of them great men keep in the shade and their ways are humble; but, when opportunity offers, they rise to the highest point of perfection. (Chau—i-ting-koo, Book 9th page 6.)

(3) The secret of making knots with cords (nets) to fish with, and traps to catch birds, was revealed to man by the character Lee ☰☰ (Chau-i-ting-koo, Book 3, page 104.) The character Lee is composed of the double sign of fire placed one after the other thus, ☰ 離 下 fire below, ☰ 離 下 fire above. (Chou-ting-koo, Book 3 page 104.)
The art of counting also comes from these mysterious symbols. We are aware that the numbers used in the binary system of numeration require but two figures, 0 and 1, to represent

Not only the science of the present, but that of the future is concealed within the forms of the sacred characters. The prophet of the Wha-seu river is a necromancer who reads the future destiny of the world in the lines of its mysterious features, in the fibres of the sacred plants, in the footsteps of the birds of heaven printed on the slime of the sea shore. Everything under the heavens and above earth, the seas, the lakes, the clouds, the mountains are, for him, as the book of fate, which has been skilfully written and opened for his information by an almighty artist.

The Ruling Power in China. The result of this strange conception of truth is easily perceived. Since the shape of a character has been settled by *Heaven* himself, each line, each stroke has in itself an authority which cannot be disputed. Add a character, a radical to the Dictionary, there is a revolution in the faith and in the Empire. Writing is sacred. Whoever shall be so impious as to throw on the floor a sheet written on, shall be punished soon or late, by *Heaven*, with the loss of his eyesight. Although a waste, it should have been religiously burned. The souls of the dead survive in their writings, and wise men, in the evening, consign to paper the resumé of their good actions, and they commit the same to the flames, so that *Heaven* may be more surely informed. While dying, the martyrs write with their blood, the ghosts, the spirits above

all the numbers; in this system, a figure placed to the left of an other, represents a unity two times stronger. In this way numbers which we designate ordinarily by 1, 2, 3, 4, 5, 6, 7, 8, 9, 10 &c., would be designated by 1, 10, 11, 100, 101, 110, 111, 1000, 1001, 1010, &c. The illustrious Leibnitz while engaged in comparing the system of numeration of the Chinese as given by the 64 Hexagrams of Foh-he, or the 8 trigrams of the Pah-kwa combined in pairs, to other systems of European origin, found that these symbols are nothing but the 64 first numbers of the system which has 2 for basis, but interverted. For if we represent the unity by —————— and the nought by —— ——, and if we agree to write the units of the various orders not from right to left, but from below up, as the noughts, placed to the left of a number, do not change its value, we find that the Chinese symbols superposed in 64 horizontal lines, as hereunder given, can be interpreted in the following way:

Chinese symbols.	Translation in binary system.	Value in the decimal system.
☰	000,000	0
☱	000,001	1
☲	000,010	2
☳	000,011	3
☴	000,100	4

and so on.

(21)

write, without intermittence, the chronicles of the planets. On his throne,

The table of the sixty-four symbols, as found in Y-king, is hereunder given. Under these symbols is their translation in the binary system, as we wouldwrite it, and to the right of these, is their value in known figures.

	63		24		39		2		9		30
111111		011000		100111		000010		001001		011110	
	23		29		45		7		13		14
010111		011101		101101		000111		001101		001110	
	55		52		15		4		50		5
110111		110110		001111		000100		110010		000101	
	61		54		43		3		21		10
111101		110110		101011		000011		010101		001010	
	25		51		49		32		34		62
011001		110011		110001		100000		100010		111110	
	41		0		6		33		16		22
101001		000000		000110		100001		010000		010110	
	57		58		46		28		56		36
111001		111010		101110		011100		111000		100100	
	18		59		11		40		8		44
010010		111011		001011		101000		001000		101100	
	60		47		27		20		48		19
111100		101111		011011		010100		110000		010011	
	53		38		12		31		1		42
110101		100110		001100		011111		000001		101010	
	35		37		17		26					
100011		100101		010001		011010					

the Emperor writes commentaries on the sacred books. Among the people the first rank has been assigned to those who the best understand the mysterious Symbols; and here is, at once, a whole nation of learned people who, according to their respective examinations, are distributed in sections of Illiterates, Bachelors, Licentiates, Doctors, &c. in the same manner other people are divided in Proletaries, Plebeians, Patricians, &c. Hence also one of the rewards promised by *Heaven* to virtuous men, that their descendants shall obtain the grade of Doctor to the third generation.

Those who have *graduated* form the class well known in China under the name of *Literati*. Living among themselves, without any apparent sign of power, they govern the Empire with a rod of iron. *The point of their pen is sharper than the edge of a sword*, is a common saying among the lower classes of Chinese. The Keün Ke-Chú, or supreme council of the Empire, sitting at Pekin, is recruited from among them. Constantly engaged in the study of the sacred books, this council is intended to advise the Emperor, not only on all the great state questions, but also on matters of minor interest; and its decisions are binding under the penalty of death. " The various ceremonies to be observed in mariage, funerals and mourning, hospitalities, religious worship, the conduct of hostilities, the shape of houses, the measure of capacity, of length, weight, are fixed by it, * * * to innovate in them is capital offence" (1).

Confucius, the commentator par excellence, is the chief and the model of the *Literati*. He is their spiritual ancestor, and they have dedicated many temples to him. His descendants compose the only nobility that is hereditary in the Empire. Around him are grouped an infinity of minor celebrities whose deeds reflect in proportion on *their* posterity. Confucius has his altars, they have theirs. So, at a certain day, the whole nation assembles in honor of the *Ancestors*. All, high and low, prostrate themselves before their images or before their names, written on paper or

---

    Leibnitz, meditating further over these symbols, the commentary of which by Confucius infortunately he had not been able to read, saw in their radicals exactly what, we have seen, they are understood to be by the Chinese, the image of the universe taken from nought by the will of God; and he argued that, as all the numbers in the binary system are derived from nought and one, so is the world which came from Nothing and of God. He became so infatuated with this idea that he advised Father Bouvet, missionary in China, to develop it before the Son of Heaven to convert him to Christianity. (See "Arithmetique par Leon Lalanne, ancien élève de l'Ecolepolytechnique, Eugenieur des Ponts et Chaussées etc., page 7, Paris 1840.)

(1) See the canon of Shun, par. 8, and the doctrine of the mean, Ch. XXVIII.

on tablets, *with the same ceremonial they observe, the same respect they show when meeting, under certain circumstances, any of those placed above them:* their father or their mother, the public officers of the Emperor or the Emperor himself. For those in power have been placed in their station by the will of *Heaven.* " *Heaven* protects the people in giving them teachers and princes. * * * Whatever the Emperor does, he does it for and by the will of *Heaven.* But the Emperor could not do everything by himself; therefore he partakes his power with others, and anything that is done by those in power is done by the command of *Heaven*" (1).

During these holy days they burn candles and perfumed sticks; a pig is killed and composes the main dish of this great communion. Are these practices idolatrous? Are they purely civil? Have they been instituted to keep, among the people, the memory of those who once were great and have been an honor to the state? Are these names written on paper considered simply as a symbol of what is good and great? Do the Chinese honor it by exterior acts as our soldiers when they salute their flag by dropping their sword before it? Are ancestors acknowledged as Gods? Or are they invoked by the Chinese as the Saints are by the Italians, the French, the Irish, the South-Americans? Although I firmly believe that the latter supposition is the correct one, I shall not undertake to settle the point by argument. I will only say that, idolatrous or not, the custom is so dear to the Chinese that they seldom give it up even after they have enbraced Christianity (2). It is in the present what is has been in the past, what it will be in the future, the stumbling block, the most serious obstacle to the propagation of our faith among them.

" Why, said the literati of Fohkien in their proclamations against foreigners, posted near Amoy, in 1868; why do you not rise to resist the dogs whom you should know, have no regards for their ancestors and their rulers; and, therefore, differ not from the most degraded brutes? Oh! you, the natives of China, listen to the teaching of the wise, discover the right from the wrong, and abstain from what is abject. A great man has said: *"Battle against innovations."* * * *

(1) Chow-king.
(2) I had a cook who was regularly attending church at the American Chapel at Amoy. Yet he would worship his ancestors tablets as another servant of mine enabled me to ascertain.

Then the author, having advised the people not to lease or sell their houses to be used as chapels by American missionaries, winds up by notifying them that, should they let their houses for that purpose, "the Literati will not fail to inform"—note well: "*to inform*—the civil officers that it "is their duty to administer the most severe punishment, without mercy, on the offender" (1).

In an other proclamation I read: "The object of this is to remove a great danger. The temple of my Ancestor Hong-Tou has long been standing * * * * and Hong-Tou's merits and renown for good morals and wisdom has spread over the seas, and it has reached Tsung-chang (a celebrated place of worship in the neighborhood of Amoy), as even the children of this place well know. How then can the vagabond Lim-Pye dare to bring any christian barbarian among us to erect a chapel * * * * and thereby do damage to my ancestor's temple. All who descend from Hong-Tou must oppose this and the indignation of the people, raised in their support, shall have no bounds. As for me I will reward with twenty Taels, in Spanish Dollars, any one, of my clan, who will succeed in taking Lim-Pye and beat the life out of him. Report this! 7th year, 10th month.

The Ruling classes oppose the Missionaries in self defence. Having risen to such a high status among their own people, it was natural that the Literati should prove jealous of any influence threatening to overthrow an order of things the fall of which must be the signal of their ruin. They have but very little to apprehend from within. The Chinese are so attached to their traditions, to their customs, that they fairly beleive their own existence as a people and their rites are inseparable. This explains why they resisted the many revolutions which have taken place in their Empire. In this they give us a spectacle unique under the sun: twenty-two reigning families, twenty-two dynasties, twenty-two revolutions, the last a most violent one, which has been marked with floods of blood, have succeeded to each other with the most singular rapidity, without apparent variations in condition of the people, in their way of living,

---

(1) The house was rented to our missionaries, soon after the issuing of that proclamation, and I had the author of the proclamation arrested after the visit which Admiral Rohan made me in 1869, and he was condemned to receive two hundred blows of the bamboo, before Dr. Talmage and forty Chinese converts. The officer who passed the sentence actually asked me to write him in the most strong terms, that he might find, in the terms of my Despatch, a justification with his superior for what he had done.

in their customs. Abroad it is different, and the experience of India, now lying at their side, almost dead as a nation, so much has it been transformed under the powerful rule of England, has taught them a terrible lesson.

The Literati fear the foreign merchant but little, for his object, wealth, is clear; and after he gets it, he generally leaves the country, and it is not likely that he will give further trouble. But in the Missionaries, who pretend to be the exclusive possessors of truth, who openly show the greatest contempt for the morals of Confucius and anything which is not foreign, they see the pioneers of a civilization from which they must have everything to fear. For if it were substituted for that of which they are the support, the power vested in their hands must pass to others. Therefore they do all they can to oppose them. Incapable of openly using force, in the face of the treaties, they have recourse to craft, and, in their ocult ways, there is nothing which they do not ressort to.

The first point in view was to keep the Missionaries from getting into the confidence of the ignorant classes. To this effect they have made them an object of terror to all. They represent them as being addicted to the most diabolical practices. They say that they kidnap and stupefy victims, that they murder children to obtain their blood, their eyes, out of which to manufacture diamond, the matrix of gold, the source of our merchant's wealth (1).

During the troubles at Tang-chow these insinuations, strange to say, found an official expression. A certain Prefect Shŭn having asked for instructions from the chief Magistrate of the District, the latter sent the following reply: "the Missionaries must not return for several months. I will refer their case to the Tsung-Lee-Yamŭn (Board of

---

(1) For a remarkably truthful representation of the animus of the ruling (literary) classes of China towards foreigners, I would refer to a book the translation of which has been published in Shanghai, last year; "DEATH BLOW TO CORRUPT DOCTRINES, AND PLAIN STATEMENT OF FACTS, PUBLISHED BY THE GENTRY AND THE PEOPLE." Montaigne, the great french philosopher of the 16th century, has written: "Les hommes sont partout et toujours les mêmes; men are everywhere and always the same. The correctness of this assertion may be proved by a reference to what has taken place in Paris, in 1572, a few weeks before the St Bartholomew The priests anxious to incite the populace against the Protestants, resorted to the same machinations. Unable to find any true ground of complaint against them they accused them of the most atrocious practices. Michelet say : *Histoire the France au 16m. Siecle—Guerres de religion. page* 394—" Le bruit courait qu'ils volaient les enfants pour les tuer et en fournir le sang à la Reine mère et au Duc d'Anjou, à qui les medecins ordonnaient, pour l'epuisement, des bains de sang humain."

Foreign Affairs in Pekin) and when the Yamûn, after consultation with the foreign Ministers, informs me that it has come to the conclusion that the Missionaries really do not abstract brains and eyes, I will myself issue a proclamation to that affect to the gentry and to the people at Tang-chow, after which the Missionaries may return * * * * (1).

Christianity in China. Confucius has skilfully adapted the most reckless impulse of the human heart to the geometrical formulas of Foh-E's revelation; a circumstance which, I fear, has too long escaped the attention of the Missionaries. I am far from advocating tactics which have found, in the estimation of those who were most interested to defend them, an eloquent disavowal, the tactics of deceit and wrong inaugurated by the Jesuits in the last century, and carried on yet by their successors of the present day. "*Pudet christum passum et crucifixum predicare.*" has been said of them by Pope Innocent X. But I firmly believe that, had the preachers of the gospel shown more tact in discussing the subject of religious reform with the Chinese, they would have been more successful. It is plain that, in the estimation of the Chinese, anything that it is not in the *Kings*, is heretic and subversive of public morals and welfare. In China every branch in the social organisation has its language. The merchants have their own; the diplomats write in a style and use terms which are most unintelligible to the merchant or the soldiers; and the philosopher, in turn, does not express his ideas like any of them; and this is so true that one may meet a Chinese and tell him that one intends studying Chinese, the first question which the professor asks is which branch of the general language one wishes to learn? that of the men in office, of the philosophers or of those engaged in trade? Therefore unless the whole Chinese language is changed, to discuss upon any subjects of morals or of religion, the style of the sacred books, or of the *Kings* must be used. This important point the Missionaries have disregarded, and their translations of the Bible, not being in the style of *Kings*, is generally considered as a very poor specimen of Chinese literature, a circumstance which prevents its being read extensively. Again the Literati contend that *truth* is eternal, and whenever it is found, in the

---

(1) His Excellency Tsang to Sun, Prefect of Tang-chow. An extract quoted in Prefect Sun's letter to Consul Medhurst, September 6, 1868—China—No. 2—1869—Correspondence presented to both houses of Parliament by command of Her Majesty.

Kings or in the *Bible* or the *New Testament*, it is God's word and should command respect. Now it is well known among those familiar with Chinese literature that there are but few of our Christian maxims which are not to be found in the Kings. Yet the preachers of the gospel have persisted in disregarding the limited relationship which exists between the morals of Christ and those of Confucius, and they have long contended with the Literati for the honor of having an exclusive conception of Divinity; and it is but lately that they have come to the conclusion to use, in their translation of the Bible, the character which, in the Kings, and the only one, I believe, in the Chinese language, conveys the idea of God (1). This childish controversy which they have kept going on, on the subject of the characters *Thien-tchu*, 天 主, God, Lord of heaven, has lasted over two hundred years. It is certain that it caused great offense to the proud Chinese who could not help seeing in the persistence of the Missionaries but an inclination to disparage them in the eyes of their own people, and, more than anything else, it has contributed in giving rise to their feeling of hatred towards the religion of Christ (2).

Another cause of drawback for the missions lies in the divisions existing in their midst. Had they made common cause in teaching the text of the gospel and, as professional men, as physicians, teachers in machematics and useful arts or trades, modestly, carefully, taking their time, moved toward the interior of the Empire, I believe that, by this time, they would have left their mark in the East. And, indeed, what would have hindered their march? Their presence would have been a blessing to the people; and as to the question of religion in itself the Literati care very little about it. In fact they are rather favorably inclined towards all religions which they consider as inoffensive superstitions and as almost indispensable substitutes for the doctrine of Confucius, which, in their pride, they believe to be quite beyong the reach of the ignorant multitude. Indeed with a view to conciliate the good wishes of the lower classes, they affect to publicly acknowledge them by making it a duty for the civil officers of the highest rank, to visit, at intervals, the places of worship which are most in favor, and especially those which belong to persuations most apt, in their estimation, to aid them in the Government of the people.

---

(1) 帝 Supreme Ruler, or Emperor above.
(2) This subject was discussed at full length by me with Lee Tajen, Governor of Formosa, in December 1869.

François Xavier, the great precursor of missionary enterprise in the East, well understood this. He almost declined discussing the doctrine of Christ; but he showed what it was capable of inspiring the man who firmly believed in it. With a spirit of heroism free from any admixture of human thoughts, and too worthy of imitation, he commenced his noble task. Alone, without guides, almost ignorant of the languages and of the places he visited, he followed at random the coast of Malabar. In India, so full of wonders, he saw only those who live far away from the towns; he spent his days with the lower people, the exiles, the parias, the little children. At sunset he would take his little bell and walk from hut to hut saying, "Good people, let us pray the Lord in Heaven!"

In this manner he traced an uninterrupted road for future comers as far as the Cormoran's cape. He planted the cross over an immense tract of land and the populations through which he passed, considering him to be God's envoy, revered and believed him. He had not to invite them; they crowded on his steps. They craved to embrace the faith of one so great of goodness and charity. François Xavier has been, on earth, a good image of Christ, and his sanctity was everywhere his safe guard.

So long as the propagators of the faith, following in this holy man's steps, circumscribed their action to the conversion of the souls and the education of the people, they were respected and in favor. Witness Ricci, who, from 1532, spent twenty-eight years at Peking, living in a house that the Emperor Ching-Tsong, 欽宗, had given to him. Adam Shall, of Cologne, in the year 1653, who superseded, as president of the college of mathematics, in Peking, the Persian astronomers, Grimaldi, Carreri, all of whom received many favors by the hands of the Emperors. But, doubtless, when, jealous one of the other, they commenced to quarrel among themselves, to intrigue one against the other in the palace, or, in general, they favored the supremacy of the Pope of Rome over the Son of Heaven, a great change took place. The Chinese lost faith in men who had failed to prove that they were true to their highest ideal. Christianity had been announced to them as a religion of peace and it had brought to them discord. It had been represented as being the communion of the humble, and the pride of Rome had shown itself in the most offensive manner to the ruling Emperor. Those who professed to be the charitable par excellence, had invited their own country to do the Chinese violence and take revenge of them.

(29)

Roused with indignation at so much hypocrysy, at the risk of losing the services which the Missionaries had rendered, and which they valued so much, (1) the Supreme Council of the Empire decided that the people should be brought to their senses and protected against the influence of a doctrine which, under the veil of charity and peace, had brought confusion and trouble in the Empire. In his explanation in ten thousand characters (Van-Tzeu-Lun), touching sixteen articles of morals which are publicly taught to the people, twice a month, the Emperor having enumerated the most objectionable sects, said:— " The religion of Europe which honors Thien-Tchu (2) is also one of those whose principles are not to be found in the Kings and are not derived from them (3). The Missionaries are acquainted with the science of Mathematics and, therefore, they have been made use of in the Empire. This every one must know."

Such was the decision of this great Emperor, and, sad as it is, and the declaration to the contrary contained in the treaties notwithstanding, it is to be feared that his successors believe yet in its wisdom, and that, for a long time to come, however powerful the intervention of the foreign powers in favor of Missionary enterprise may be, the crown of the martyrs will be the only reward which christian truth has to offer to its defenders.

TAIWAN-FOO, Island of Formosa, *January*, 1870.

(1) Among other things they made the maps of the Empire. Their atlas is in my hands.
(2) [The Lord of Heaven] two characters invented by the Missionaries and by which they have long translated the word " God."
(3) 易經 The Yh-king " book of changes," and which, I have so often quoted above, is regarded with almost universal reverence by the Chinese, both on account of its antiquity, and also the unfathonable wisdom which is supposed to lie concealed under its mysterious Symbols. As I have already said, the authorship of the Symbols (卦 Kwa), which forms the nucleus of the work, is with great confidence attributed to Foh-he or Paou-he. These consisted originally, as we have seen, of 8 trigrams, but were subsequently, by combining them in pairs, augmented to the 64 hexagrams. The work is said to have escaped destruction at the time of the burning of books, B. C. 220, in consequence of its application to purposes of divination; books of that class having being excepted. Traditions relates, however, that the three last sections by Confucius were lost about that time, and were afterwards found by a girl at the Yellow River. A long list of scholars are recorded as having distinguished themselves as expounders of the Yh-king, some by oral instructions and other by their writings. (See Notes on Chinese &c., by A. Wylie, Shanghai and London, 1867, pages 1 and 2).
I have never seen any translation of Yh-king into any European languages but Mr. Wylie states that there is one in Latin. Yh-king, antiquissimus, Sinarum Liber quem ex latina interpretatione P. Regis aliorum que ex Soc. Jesu P. P. edidit Julius Mohl. 1834, Stutsgartiae et Tubingae, 2 vol.

MEMORANDUM No. 2.

THE TWENTY FIRST OF JUNE AND THE DIPLOMACY IN PEKING.

(33)

Memorandum No 2.

THE TWENTY FIRST OF JUNE AND THE DIPLOMACY IN PEKING.

Homo sum: humani nihil a me alienum puto.
Terence.

On may passage to Shanghai, in December last, (1869) I naturally made many inquiries concerning the massacres of the 21 of June. Surprised to hear so many contradictory reports of the affair, I made up my mind to call upon a gentleman whose love for truth, for truth's sake, I well knew, and whose devotion to the cause of China I had had many opportunities to witness, and who was better situated than almost any one I knew of, to furnish a correct statement of the affair. I was not deceived in my expectations; and, indeed, the disclosures of my friend were so startling that I had no rest till he gave me a written memorandum of our interview, which I agreed to arrange for communication to my Government, while he promised to send a paper, on the same subject, to the press.

The plot. My friend said.—For the last three or four years past it has been reported, each year, that, on the 21 of June (1), there would be a general messacre of foreigners, and of this, not one of the Ministers residing at Peking, must have been ignorant. Our Doplomats have equally been aware of the views expressed, nearly fifteen or eighteen months ago, by Tseng-Kwo-fan 曾國藩 and Le Hung-chang, in answer to an Imperial edict submitting to their judgment certain questions, and that these two high dignitaries agreed in saying that, although nothing could be more desirable than to resist foreign demands, the nation was not ready to fight, and that, therefore, it would be advisable to wait. —— The question of war being thus set a side by the united advice of the chiefs of the army, the extreme party decided to seek from a popular uprising the execution of its programme. In consequence detailed instructions were sent to all the parts of the Empire, and the signal was to

---

(1) The day had been fixed, it is said, by their fortune tellers.

come from Nanking. It was General Cheng Kwo-joui 陳國瑞, who, on his return from Sze-chuen, 四川, at the end of last April, was intrusted with the task of inciting the people. In this he failed owing to the prudence and energy of Vice Roy Ma, 馬新貽, who ordered the principal chiefs of the movement to be seized and put to death (1). Cheng Kwo-joui 陳國 瑞, defeated on this score, hastened to Tientsin, where he arrived during the first days of June, and lost no time in preparing, by means of stormy public meetings, for the melancholy tragedy of the 21st of June, (2).

Tientsin, like all the other towns in the interior, was covered with placards, calling the people to arms against the kidnappers of children and reproducing, in the most violent language, the old stories of the worst times, viz: that the sisters of charity were in the habit of taking out the eyes and hearts of the children wherewith to make a hateful medecine. At the present moment, I simply narrate the facts as they took place; the Count de Rochechouart, in a memorandum sent to the Tsung-Lee Yamên, and published by the newspapers, a few months ago, established, with great force of logic, the culpability of these great criminals, and I need not add a word to what he said in that occasion. Therefore I come to the 21st of June:—

(1) Mr. Consul Medhust had called the attention of Mr. Wade to the occurrence saying: "That it was quite within the compass of possibility that the act had been committed in revenge for the active and determined measures which Ma adopted against the military students of Gan-king-fu with a view to compel them to produce the two ring leaders in the attack upon the Missionary establishments of that city." The assasination of prominent members of the Provincial authorities is entirely foreign to the temper and spirit of Chinese people, and almost unprecedented in the modern history of China. It is almost evidence of the excitement which must have existed at the time. Mr. Medhust fully understood the significance of the act, for he wrote to Mr. Wade: "If this hypothesis be correct, the incident must have a deep significance in the eyes of the Chinese at the present conjuncture of affairs. The mere fact that so high and influential an officer as the Vice-Roy of the Two Kiang Provinces can be thus sacrificed on account of his leaning towards foreigners will certainly create an agitation in the minds of all classes. It will have the effect of causing the well-disposed towards us to lose heart, while it will embolden those amongst the officials and Literati who do favour foreign relations to persist in their efforts to incense the mass of the population against us. In any event the consequences as regards any Missionaries, French or British, who may at present be residing at Nankiog and in the neighbouring districts are likely to be anything but agreeable."

(2) See Mr. Rochechouart's despatches in which he states that, in his journey from the central provinces to Tientsin, Cheng Kwo-joui's route may be traced by a succession of outrages on Foreigners which followed on his wake. See also Mr. Wade's despatches to his Government on the subject of Cheng Kow-joui's connection with the massacre.

The 21st of June. On the morning of that day, numerous groups had assembled before the Consulate of France; vociferations were heard, stones were thrown from all sides, the shops were closed in the city, and the gong called all the citizens to arms to burn the Consulate of France and the church, and to massacre foreigners. Mr. Fontanier, the French Consul, from this moment, realized the extent of the danger. He knew full well that he could not, in any event, expect help from those who had organized the movement; but he had known Chung-How 崇厚, for many years. The perfect urbanity with which this officer had always treated all foreigners, the marks of sympathy which he had always shown towards them, had left in his mind the conviction that this high dignitary would interpose in the trouble. It is then that he wrote his letter to the Chargé d'Affaires of France, dated several hours before his death, and, if my information is correct, in it, he expressed the conviction that Chung-How would disperse the mob, and that order would be entirely restored in the afternoon (1). But he was fated to learn, two hours later, that not only Chung-How would not come, in person, to the Consulate, but that he would not even send a single soldier to protect him, and that he would remain concealed from the sight of all in his Yamên during the whole time that the butchery should last.

Before going on with this recital, I must remark that I do not hesitate to say that Chung-How has not been, for a moment, in complicity with the Prefect and the Sub-Prefect; but I am equally convinced that, if he had done his duty, his heart would not have failed at the most critical moment. If he had gone officially to the Consulate, as he should have done, the massacre would have been prevented. I cannot better compare his conduct than to that of a Commander of a war vessel, who, while on shore, being informed that a mutiny had broken out on board and that the sailors are murdering their officers, will not go on board for fear of being murdered also. Such an officer would be brought before a court martial, and, the least that could happen to him, would be to be degraded as unworthy of holding any future command (2). Therefore I deeply regret to see that Chung-How, sheltered by the bill of indemnity which the French Minister has spontaneously accorded to him, has

(1) See the Consul's Despatch which has been published in England.
(2) This is Chinese law.

received, as a premium of encouragement, a nonination as Ambassador. The letter of poor Fontanier, in my opinion, establishes but one fact, viz: that he understood very little the Chinese, and that he had misplaced his confidence; but, far from furnishing an argument in favor of this dignitary, as the French Chargé d'Affaires thinks it does, to me it proves his guilt.

It has been said by Chung-How that Mr. Fontanier had twice fired with his revolver at him, in his Yamên, and that this attempt against his life had been, in some way, the signal of the massacre. But besides the fact that this allegation is contrary to good sence (because the only hope that, then, remained to Mr. Fontanier was of the support of Chung-How, and, this person being off the scene, there was simply death in the background), I shall here affirm that, in the course of an interview between Chung-How and myself, a fact with which I have acquainted both Messrs. Rochechouart and Wade, His Excellency acknowledged that the French Consul did not fire at him, but he had been compelled to accuse him of it in order to shield himself in his relations with the Emperor (1).

We are all aware that the infortunate Fontanier had a violent and irascible disposition, upon which they found a report that, in the Yamên of Chung-How, in a fit of ungovernable rage, he had smashed every thing within his reach. In support of this assertion, they alleged the testimony of his Chinese servant who had accompanied him that day to the Superintendent of the three ports; but this same servant, being questioned by others, has declared that he did not go into the Yamên, but waited for his master at the door. How then could he have seen what took place within? I can understand and admit that Mr. Fontanier, on going out of the Yamên, became almost frantic with rage, and that he fired on the Sub-Prefect whom he saw applauding the deeds of the mob. I feel deeply in my heart what must have passed in his, when he saw that Chung-How abandoned him, and he had to confess to himself that there was no more hope. It is said that, at this juncture,

---

(1) * * * "The blow struck, he tells a story which must be received with great caution, to wit, that Mr. Fontanier came armed to his Yámen, abused him, fired a pistol, if not at him, in his presence, similarly assaulted the magistrate, and was consequently killed by the people."
Mr. Lay proves that in one important particular he has contradicted himself. On the 22nd he affirmed that Mr. Fontanier has been killed close to him, and that he had his remains in his Yámen. On the 23rd Mr. Fontanier's body was recovered by Mr. Lay from the river. (Mr. Wade to his Government).

His Excellency offered to our Consul to conceal him in his Yamên, pledging himself to save his life. But our true representative, on that day, remembered that he had left at the Consulate the Interpreter of the French Legation, Mr. Thomassin and his young wife; moreover that the Sisters of charity, the church, and, finally, the Flag of France had been entrusted to his honor; and, being unable to do anything for them where he was, he went to die with them.

At the time Mr. Fontanier was withdrawing, dispair in his heart, from the Yamên of Chung-How, that functionary did not even condescend to escort him to the first interior court, and it was a few seconds after that, while passing the door of the exterior court, he received his first wound, a thrust of a spear in the right side, and, in a moment, his garments were covered with blood. The Count de Rochechouart is well aware of this fact, which took place a few steps from the man who, a little later, was to be sent as Ambassador to offer the apology of China to and reasure the French Government as to the intention of the cabinet of Peking. The six hundred troops armed and drilled by English and French officers during the last few years, at the request of Chung-How, were not sent by him to interfere for the re-establishment of order. It is said they were at the Consulate and at the house of the Sisters, giving efficient aid to the murderers in their bloody work. The Sub-Prefect of Tientsin was officially on the spot where he encouraged, to the utmost of his power, those ferocious beasts set loose by himself and his superior, the Prefect; finally the General Chên Kwo-joui, in full uniform, on horseback, in the midst of the people, was commander, *de facto*, of this altogether new kind of expedition. All agree in saying that from eight to ten thousand men took part directly or indirectly in this work of monstrous iniquity.

No one will contradict these facts; I give them to you as absolutely true; far, then, from attacking the conduct or character of one who is no more, of Fontanier, let us lay this outrage at the door of those to whom it belongs: the Imperial Government of China, and bow, with respect, before this tomb all covered with blood.

You do not expect that I should begin again the recital of the horrors of that day; that I should show you the victims cut to pieces and their mangled remains thrown into the river; that I should describe to you the tortures inflicted upon the sisters of charity; that I should let you see the clenched hands which struck the children of the orphanage, and the still warm pieces of flesh for which those ferocious beasts were struggling in order that they might parade, carrying them about the town on the end of their pikes. The spectacle of these remains, which we have buried, with pious respect, on the site of the Consulate of France, will always remain present to my memory.

The day of the funerals, the Chargé d'Affaires of France and of England could hardly restrain their tears, and the French Admiral, in indignant language, gave expression to what all felt at the bottom of their hearts. Alone the Chinese remained indifferent. His Excellency Tseng Kwo-fan was absent from the ceremony. He did not think it needful for him, Imperial Commissioner, who had been appointed to settle this outrage, to give us, by his presence, a justly expected token of sympathy or consolation. The new Prefect and Sub-Prefect disappeared before the beginning of the funeral. As to Chung-How, he well played his role of friend: he affected great grief and was present to the last. President de Thou, the most cowardly man of France, well said, when he quoted those words of Louis XI, in connection with Charles IX, a few days after the St. Bartholomew: "Qui nescit dissimulare, nescit regnare."

Let us draw, now, a veil over this lamentable tragedy, as Count de Rochechouart justly called it, and let us pursue our investigation into the conduct and the acts of the local authorities of Tientsin and of the cabinet of Peking during the days that followed this horrible deed.

The acts of the local authorities of Tientsin and of the Cabinet of Peking, after the Massacre.

On the 23rd, the local authorities of Tientsin, frightened at what had taken place the day before, and wishing to justify their conduct before the Emperor, should the pressure exerted by the foreign Ministers render it necessary, proceeded to arrest from fifteen to eighteen Chinese catholics, who were tortured, to make them confess that the sisters of charity were in the habit of taking out the eyes and hearts of children wherewith to make their diabolic medecine. Of these fifteen or eighteen unfortunates, three are dead, and the others have been returned to us covered with wounds and in a desperate condition. Mr. de Rochechouart will not contradict this; for it is himself who, having with threats on his lips, required their liberation, established the fact. The populace, so far as I know, had nothing to do with this iniquitous act, which is so intimately connected with the murder of the day before. They have carefully omitted making it known to the public and to the Governments; and indeed, I admire the singular facility with which certain people pass over these occurrences, so that, without compromissing themselves, they may persuade our Governments to believe on these ridiculous terms of satisfaction which Chung-How, the involuntary yet the real author of the tragedy of the 21st of June, is going to submit to them.

At the first news of the massacre of Tientsin the members of the Department of Foreign Affairs, justly alarmed at the consequences that might follow, went, in a body, to the various Ministers to express the sorrow which these events had caused them, and to propose for the signature of the Emperor, a decree appointing Tseng Kwo-fan Imperial Commissioner to open an inquiry into these events (1). The decree dwelt with complacency on the misdeeds of the Missionaries and of the Christians, and attributed the massacre to the alleged pistol-shot of Mr. Fontanier. Two days later General Chen Kwo-joui arrived at Peking, where he was received in triumph, and where he resumed his luxurious and dissipated mode of life, without even so much as being troubled by questions. The Chargé d'Affaires of France, it is true, clearly established his guilt, and, in indignant despatches, demanded his execution; but they did not deign to examine into the matter, even for form's sake.

Tseng Kwo-fan, on the other side, slowly prepared to leave Pao-ting-foo for Tientsin, where he arrived in the early days of July with a few thousand men. But he was so sick that he was almost unable to fulfil the mission which had been entrusted to him. The Count de Roche-chouart, invited by the Tsung-lee-yamen to go to Tientsin in order to, in concert with the Commissioner, arrest the guilty parties and settle this horrible affair amicably and in conformity to the laws of justice,

---

(1) After the St. Bartholemew in 1572, the authors of the massacre were those who most reproved it. "Charles IX lui même craignit l'effet de la tête de Coligny arrivant à Rome. Il ordonna au gouverneur de Lyon de l'arrêter au passage. ......Un jacobin breton, Masset, dans son histoire de son ordre, imagina affirma qu'un saint homme, directeur de Catherine de Medicis et de Diane de Poitiers, l'Evêque de Lisieux, Hennuyer, avait empêché le massacre dans cette ville. Le Jesuite Maimbourg a reproduit ce recit. Malheureusement les registres de la ville de Lisieux établissent le contraire. Ce fut le magistrat qui empêcha l'effusion du sang. et nullement l'Evêque, alors absent, et d'ailleurs ardent persecuteur." (J. Michelet. La Ligue et Henry IV, notes, pages 478 and 479).

lost not a minute in coming to confer with the colleague assigned to him; but these conferences were not to last long. During the fifteen or twenty days that Mr. de Rochechouart remained in Tientsin, he saw Tseng Kwo-fan but twice; the first time when, on his arrival, he called upon the Commissioner, and, the second time, when Tseng Kwo-fan returned his call, at the English Consulate, then the Consulate of France. And, during their solemn interviews, this comical remark was made, unique expression of the feelings and views of this Imperial Commissioner: "The unfortunate affair of Tientsin has been caused by the ignorance of the people, I am going to propose to have them educated by our *Literati*," —the most hostile and vicious class in the whole Empire—"this will take several years, say two or three, after which we need not fear a renewal of such scenes (1)." But as to an inquiry, it was not mentioned; as to arrests, not one was made.

While this was going on, the true murderers of the 21 of June had escaped, some to Shan-tung 山東, others to Peking itself. Tseng Kwo-fan, being too sick to acquit himself, with the desired promptness, of the mission entrusted to him, one of the member of the Board of Foreign Affairs was dispatched to Tientsin. But he also found himself in such a weak state, when he arrived, that he had to postpone *sine die* the inquiry which was to be made.

Mr. de Rochechouart returns to Peking. In disgust Mr. de Rochechouart made up his mind to return to Peking, having secured previously, however, that the victims of the 21st of June should be interred in a Catholic cemetery.

We were then at the beginning of August, and more than six weeks had passed since the crime had been committed without any one thinking of beginning the trial of the murderers. The Cabinet of Peking, knowing well that all impressions are blunted with time, conformed to its traditional policy and was gaining time, (2) spending weeks in endless communications. It would be a curious and interesting

---

(1) In two or three years it will be too late to pacify China. The chiefs of the war party, feeling that they are ready, will demand the general expulsion of the barbarians.

(2) The central Government was making preparations to resist by force any demands that might be made by France. Now they have Prussian steel guns and French mitrailleuse, in Foochow, American breach loaders, in Amoy, and they are drilling every day everywhere.

(41)

reading than that of the despatches exchanged between the Legations and the Chinese Ministers, together with the narratives of their interviews. All of them simply referred to the imprudence of Missionaries, to the kidnapping of children, to the branding with infamy of the attempt of Mr. Fontanier on the life of Chung-How, and to setting forth the turbulent character of the people of Tientsin.

Confidential Edict of the Emperor to 13 Vice-Roys. While this was going on, his Imperial Majesty was addressing to all the Vice-Roys and Governors of Provinces the following confidential Edict.

"The Emperor has ordered Tseng Kwo-fan, Vice-Roy of the Province of Chi-li, to proceed to Tientsin to settle the affair relating to the troubles between the people of that city and the Christians, and this officer has, according to his instructions, begun an inquiry, of which the results promise to be satisfactory. Meanwhile these circumstances have suggested to the Emperor the following considerations; the Chinese Christians are to day the object of violent attacks on all sides, and foreigners are profiting by it to impose on us, by means of their war vessels, and, in the way of compensations, terms altogether extravagant. China should not be the first to commence hostilities; but quietly, she ought to prepare to defend herself, and that without loss of time; and if, through the inconsiderate conduct of foreigners, disorders should occur at any ports of the Empire, their rebellious demands are not to be submitted to at any price whatever. It is not well to wait for rain before repairing the roof; thus it is desirable, at present, to take an account of the means of defence which the different coast provinces possess. To this effect the Emperor instructs the Vice Roys and Governors of provinces (here follow thirteen names) to proceed actively and without delay to the instruction of troops and review of the organizations. They should heartily devote themselves to this and bring all their ressources to bear. They should also beware of making any reports which do not express the exact truth, to the end that China, being well prepared, need have nothing to fear. Meanwhile the Emperor invites the high officials (just named) to address him a detailed report of the actual state of the means of defence in their respective territories. This decree is hastened by special courier who is to travel six hundred li per day. Respect this!"

Now here is the reply made to the Emperor, a few weeks afterward, by one of the Vice-Roys, the one most enlightened and kindly disposed towards foreigners. From this document you may imagine what those, who are not exactly our friends, may have written.

"The decree of the Emperor, with reference to putting in a state of defence the coasts of Fukien, Chekiang and Formosa, has come into the hands of his humble subject, and he desires to submit, very respectfully, to his sacred Majesty, several general considerations, and to make him acquainted with a few things in the Provinces under his jurisdiction.

"In the opinion of the humble Minister of your Majesty the troubles of Tientsin are only the consequence of griefs accumulating for years, and not an affair of a day or of a night (1); and, to begin with, it is only too certain that the Missionaries, under pretext of coming to teach virtue to our people, preach to them the most perverse and corrupt doctrines, and their converts are recruited from the least respectable part of the population; they impudently violate our laws and our customs, under cover of their names of Christians, and finally, they have forever arrayed against them all that is honest in the Empire. As to accusing them of kidnapping children, to take out their hearts and eyes, your subject admits that it is impossible, and that such reports are without foundation (2).

(1) How can any one say, after this, that the Tientsin massacre was a simple riot? It is true, Prince Kung wrote to Mr. Rochechouart: "The Tientsin affair was but a movement of the people excited for one day. It will not take long to dispose of it and relations will be more friendly than ever." Lord Granville who probably had not read the answer of the Vice-Roy to the Emperor, quoted above, wrote Mr. Wade in the same sense, under date of the 6th of October he said: "It was a great satisfaction to Her Majesty's Government to learn by your telegram just received, that in the three months that had elapsed between its date and the date of the massacre nothing had occured calculated to show that that tragedy was likely to be repeated in other parts of China, or to warrant the opinion, perhaps not unnaturally entertained on the spot in the first moments of alarm, that it indicated a determination on the part of the Chinese authorities and people to exterminate foreigners in general." But later Mr. Wade changed his mind and said: "The most active of the rioters would of course be those who had something to gain by it, and I think with Mr. Lay that the attitude of the community and the badness of the weather had much to say in the immunity of the British settlement from molestation."

(2) Mr. Wade wrote after the massacre: "I feel bound to combat the impression, which is that of many foreigners, that this discontent was sheerly the work of the authorities or of the influential classes. The Chinese, as their law-books show, do believe that by spells and drugs kidnappers can bewitch whom they will (*vide* Inclosure 33). The educated classes are, in all that belongs to physiological knowledge, as ignorant and superstitions as the common people. I think it as likely as not that the Tientsin authorities did believe, as the people believed, that children were being kidnapped, and that for the purposes alleged; nor would this conclusion be

Finally your subject ought to mention the violent measures taken, at every step, by foreigners, and their pretensions to keep our population under the menace of their war vessels, as having contributed to increase their hatred of the foreign element. In a word all their wicked deeds and griefs together make up the actual situation.

France has more especially prepared, by her political acts, what has taken place to day (1). She will, therefore, certainly not allow to pass unnoticed the murder of her Consul, of her Missionaries, the destruction of her temples and the tearing of her Flag. Consequently we ought to expect to see her war vessels coming to back her foolish demands. Therefore your Majesty was well inspired when he made us prepare to repel the aggressors. The humble servant of your Majesty, understanding very well the idea of the Emperor that *the defence should be secret, so that, at a given moment, he can dispose of the fate of foreigners as his Majesty pleases,*(2) has given the most precise and confidential orders to have the troops armed, provisioned and drilled, and, in concert with the Tartar-General, has taken all necessary steps for the defence of the Capital of the Province." * * * * * * Here follows, in long phraseology, the names of the chiefs on whom they may depend, the steps which they propose to take, and the present state of the ports of Foochow, Amoy and Formosa, details which have very little interest for the subject which occupies us. The preamble is more than sufficient to inform us how the crime of Tientsin is regarded by the highest authorities of the Empire, and the friendly feelings professed towards us by the representatives who are most in confidence of the Government that sits at Peking. You will not forget neither that the author of this representation to the throne is one of the Governors General who belonged to the peace party, and one who has given us, at all times, the least equivocal testimony of sympathy.

---

shaken if it were shown that, as some declare, they took pains to extort a confession from those who have been brought before them as guilty of kidnapping. It is the habit of their Courts, in half the serious cases they try, to strain the evidence to secure a conviction."

(1) Lord Granville has expressed almost the same views; he said, " * * *; but they cannot conceal from themselves that the calamity has been the result of a system, which they have always deprecated as dangerous and impolitic and which they have long foreseen might lead to events such as they now deplore." My own opinion is that the massacre has not been the result of the system, but that the system has been a pretext for the outrage.

(2) This is terribly illustrative of Chinese ways and should not pass unnoticed by the foreign powers.

While this was going on, an army of nearly 50,000 men, with a large force of artillery, was concentrated in that city, or within a radius of thirty miles. This display of force was intended, so it was said, to frighten the rioters;

Wonderful skill exhibited by the cabinet of Pekin, after the massacre.

but it does not appear that these troops understood their role, for, up to the end of September, the merchants of Tientsin, confined, as it were, to the British concession, could not do business in that same city of Tientsin, without being exposed to daily insults. Yet Mr De Rochechouart, animated with a sincere desire to settle this affair in an honorable way for his country, in conformity with his programme, according to which the murderers would have been executed on the ruins of our consular and catholic establishments, was active in his negociations, and received, by the middle of September, the news of the appointment of a new Imperial Commissioner and his arrival at Tientsin. This one came to us from Shanghai; he was the Governor of the province of Kiang-su, His Excellency Tsing 丁 寳 楨.

When I recall my impressions and endeavor coolly to judge of this period, I am confounded at the tranquillity with which our Ministers had assisted at all these scenes, and the unparalleled credulity with which they listened to the fables which were dealt out to them day by day, and the hopes which they were led to cherish. At all events, they saw, in the arrival of the Governor of Kiang-su a living and sure proof that they were nearing the end of their task. But this time, again, our diplomats had not made due allowance for oriental duplicity. They had forgotten the too well known and distinctive characteristics of the agents of the power that now reigns at Peking.

His Excellency Ting showed due diligence in ordering arrests in all quarters of the city of Tientsin; but the persons arrested, having no connection whatever with the 21st of June, were almost immediately released on the payment of a heavy fine. In one word, this first phase of the mission of Ting Foutai may be summed up thus: "a forced tax levied on the population of Tientsin in aid of the Imperial treasury in distress." On the other hand, the moral effect of these measures on the people may be well imagined, if we consider that these imposts were demanded as means of satisfying the claims of the foreigners.

Chinese diplomacy was very able indeed at this juncture; for it succeeded in persuading the French representative that they were engaged in arresting the assasins of our Consul, of our Sisters of charity and of our citizens. It made the Chinese, whom it was ruining, believe that it was doing it to satisfy our demands and thereby avoiding more serious complications; the guilty authorities, that they should be neither tried nor punished as accomplices in the crime; finally, the Emperor, that it was gaining for him the time necessary for His Excellency Li-Hung-chang, 李鴻章, whose nomination as Vice-Roy of Chi-li had been already decided, to come with his Honan braves, troops armed and disciplined in foreign style, and acustomed to fatigues and fighting by six years of constant warfare.

Long before the news of the nomination and of the arrival of Li-Hung-chang at Tientsin had transpired among the populace, it was communicated to Mr. de Rochechouait. But he refused to credit it, *because the Tsung-li-yamen had told him the contrary*. When, two days later, it became impossible to ignore so evident a fact, they caused it to be said to our representative by his Interpreter ad interim that the Vice-Roy Li was simply coming to establish himself with his army on the frontier of Chi-li, to protect this province against a possible invasion of Musulmans (1). So simple an explanation satisfied everybody, appearing altogether natural; but, three days after, they took advantage of the death of Ma to insert in the Peking Gazette the nomination of Li-Hung-chang to the Vice-Royalty of Chi-li, and that of Tseng Kwo-fan to the Vice-Royalty of Nankin. It became necessary, then, to explain this step, which the cabinet of Peking found no difficulty in doing; they gave our Minister to understand that they were very much dissatisfied with Tseng Kwo-fan, in that he had acquitted himself very badly of the mission with which he had been charged. That Li-Hung-chang would go and entirely change the aspect of affairs, being a man of well known energy. Nothing can give an idea of the satisfaction with which this communication was received. The Minister was perfectly convinced that this time the affair would be settled according to his wishes on the arrival of Vice-Roy Li, and that the fault of all these delays was entirely due to the secret hostility of Tseng Kwo-fan; and he certainly would have taxed with folly,

---

(1) It may be well to say here that the Musulmans were then in the Kanseu, a province lying some seven hundred miles west from Tientsin.

if not impertinence, whoever would have refused to believe implicitily this so natural explanation furnished, of its own accord, by the Cabinet of Peking.

The arrival of Li-Hung-chang at Tientsin did not at all have the effect of hastening the departure of Tseng Kwo-fan, who had acquitted himself so poorly of his duties. But a despatch of Prince Kung to Mr. de Rochechouart, dated 15th October, a despatch which recited the rediculous, not to say shameful, terms of reparation which were granted to us, plainly informed this diplomatic Agent that the opinion of Tseng Kwo-fan had prevailed in the counsels of the Emperor, and that the decrees given were at his instance.

One would have thought that, after this new deception, our Minister would have drawn the conclusion that, in these Eastern countries, one must not be too credulous; far from that, he was satisfied with his work was almost charmed with the despatch of the 15th of October; and, in' a word, he considered the matter as settled.

Yet, in the beginning of September, while the Ministers of France and England, in spite of all the warnings given to them, failed to modify their opinion, that the affair of Tientsin is a local and accidental occurrance, which it is important to pass over for the better preservation of our future relations with China, an other Imperial Edict, secret and confidential was circulated. In it the Count de Rochechouart was treated in the most off hand manner, his demands being taxed with exaggeration and folly; and it finally ended by stating that they had determined to resist them at any price. This curious document has been transmitted for their information, from Tientsin, to the Legations of France and England; It has been circulated among the populace at Tientsin, that same populace which was represented to us as being turbulent, and which the Chinese Government was really anxious to bring back to better feelings towards us! At the same time, fans were distributed and publicly sold in Tientsin, on which the massacre of Mr. Fontanier, of his chancellor and of Mrs. Thomassin was represented. In the middle of the card was the Sub-Prefect who was present at this bloody spectacle, a smile on his lips, applauding the crowd.

Now what were the Chinese doing in the other parts of the Empire? They were conforming strictly to the instructions of the Emperor, to the instructions contained in the secret Edict which I have quoted above.

They were buying everywhere field pieces of the latest patern, mitrailleuses, needle guns, and, what will appear wonderful, is that we were all aiding them in making these purchases made under the eyes of the Legations, of the Consuls, who had all been notified, and not a protest came from them, not a demand for explanation (1).

Sacrificia ad portenda. Finally the great day of reparation came. Some twenty miserable beings, who had been fanaticized in advance, sacrified themselves to their masters (2). Large sums of money were paid to their families, public feasts were offered to them, and they were led to the place of execution, as of old, the ancient sacrificers dragged to the axe the pure victims devoted to appease the anger of the Gods, that is, covered with flowers and sacred fillets.

Contrary to Chinese law, which requires the heads of felons to be exposed to public gaze, for certain number of days, in wooden cages, the heads of these patriot-martyrs, piously sewed to the necks from which they had been detached, to satisfy old prejudices and ancient traditions, were, with the bodies to which they belonged, buried in ground selected beforehand. The people of Tientsin were so impressed by their heroic abnegation that they lately asked to be allowed to erect a monument in their honor. On the other side the cabinet of Peking was honorably handing over to Mr. de Rochechouart what it had agreed to pay viz: for the life of our Consul, 30,000 taels,—for that of his chancellor, 20,000; for Mr. and Mrs. Thomassin, $50,000 &c. &c., Sum total, 250,000 Tails. The life of each one had been valued in a liberal manner.

As to our consular and catholic establishments, the Chargé d'Affaires of France had himself presented his bills for them; and it is but just to say that the sum was paid without discussion. May be it is not without interest to mention that these indemnities must be paid by the adminis-

---

(1) The importation of foreign arms at Amoy and Foochow by the Chinese Government has been enormous.

(2) This is a custom in China for an officer, even of small rank, to send a servant or a slave of his to appear for him before the judge by whom he has been summoned, and the practice has force of law. However I was not aware that in capital offences even a high officer would be dispensed from appearing. He would not in case of treason. But very likely the murder of a few barbaricus was not considered a very serious offence.

tration of the foreign Customs; in other words, it is the money of foreigners which is given for the life of foreigners (1).

The foregoing is what Chung-How has been told to announce to France, that is, provided one of his instructions is to tell the truth to the Government to which he is accredited.

As to myself, when the news of the departure of that Ambassador, at the instance of the french Representative himself, reached me, the flush of shame mounted to my brow, and I may affirm that the feeling of indignation in which every foreigner residing in this country partakes, has been freely brought to the notice of Mr. de Rochecouart. That the situation of this Diplomatic Agent may have been more than delicate, no one of us will deny, but he had a very simple part to act, and *that was to do nothing.*

Conclusion. The affair of Tientsin does not exclusively interest France; it interests all human kind; and it is incontestable that a feeling of self preservation should have compelled the other powers to espouse our quarrel. By accepting this sad bargain, by receiving this sordid money, and chiefly by distributing the same at once, we have almost approved the decision of the cabinet of Peking, and we have closed the case.

I do not wish to put Count de Rochechouart on his trial; but I would put on trial the policy he followed; that this Agent, justly troubled and sorely grieved by the misfortunes of his country, seeing France devastated, ruined, has made up his mind to avoid, at all cost, all complications, and it may be war, we can easely believe. But, by doing that, he has nevertheless committed a fault, the consequences of which are incalculable.

(1) On the 29th of December Lord Granville wrote to Mr. Wade: "Although the immediate danger by which the maintenance of friendly relations between foreign nations and China was threatened may, it is to be hoped, be considered to be removed by the satisfaction tendered to, and accepted by the French Chargé d'Affaires in atonement of the massacre of French subjects at Tientsin in the month of June last, yet it is impossible for Her Majesty's Government to accept the tardy and reluctant consent of the Chinese Government to do justice in a case in which the feelings of all Christian nations were so enlisted, as sufficient to efface the displeasure which they have felt in regard to these matters. Although the victims of these attempts are almost exclusively French, it cannot be denied that such deeds reveal the existence of dangers which menace without distinction all foreigners residing in China. It is by considering their interests as common in these countries of the extreme East that the European Powers can arrive at securing to their countrymen the guarantees and the security stipulated for in the Treaties.

And in politics a fault is worse than a crime. My only hope, to-day, is that public opinion, enlightened as to those sad events, will remember that she is mistress of governments and derectress of their politics, and that Republican France will keep intact the honor of the country, if she can not preserve her influence; that she will send back this Ambassador as unworthy of negociating with her, and that she will plainly tell Peking that it is more than daring to send her such a Representative." * * * *

* * *December,* 1870.

MEMORANDUM No. 3.

A TRIP OVERLAND FROM FOOCHOW TO AMOY.

Memorandum No. 3.

A TRIP OVERLAND FROM FOOCHOW TO AMOY.

3rd to 9th January, 1871.

> J'étais là; telle chose m'advint
> La Fontaine.

The following are extracts of a Journal kept by W. Lee Sibbald Esquire, the able Interpreter of the Imperial Maritime Customs at Foochow, during a trip of seven days taken in January last. It will be read with interest considering that the Massacre of Tientsin took place on the 21st of June last, and that the assault on Mr. Secretary Seward, at Woo-chang was made in December of the same year.

A Visit to the Governor General of Foo-kien and Che-kiang. Mr. Sibbald writes:—On the 1st of January 1871, I was invited by General Le Gendre, American Consul at Amoy, to call with him and Mr. Keim, a special Agent of the United States Government for the inspection of Consulates in the East, on H. E. Ying Kwei (英桂), Governor General of the two provinces of Foo-kien and Che-kiang, at his official residence, in the City of Foo-chow-foo (福州府), in the capacity of interpreter. This official is upwards of seventy years of age, and first became generally known to foreigners in his capacity of Tartar General and *ex-officio* Superintendent of Customs. He is a man of the highest rank and wears as such a red buttom of the first grade. General Le Gendre had often met him before and had had many dealings with him. Mr. Keim was of course a stranger. After usual Chinese compliments had been gone through, General Le Gendre explained to H. E., in general terms, the objects of Mr. Kiem's visit to the East. * * * H. E. re-echoed the sentiments of friendship as expressed by General Le Gendre and Mr. Kiem and said that he saw no prospect of a change in the friendly feeling existing between America and China. Mr. Kiem then gave a general sketch of his trip, stating that while en route for China, he had visited the open ports of Japan, and that since his arrival in China he had visited Peking and seen

the great Ministers of the Tsung-li-yamen (Chinese foreign office 總理
衙門); that he had been at Tientsin and Shanghai, and ascended the
great river Yang-tze.kiang 揚子江, and had experienced everywhere
the most considerate treatment; that he would, on his return to America,
inform the President of the fact, and narrate to him all that occurred
during his travels in China. This, with a few remarks on different subjects,
gives a general idea of the conversation carried on between his Excellency
and ourselves. H. E. had been notified of our contemplated trip overland
to Amoy, and had directed a small official to be in attendance on us, and
to prepare everything. * * *

Difficulty of Dealing with Chinese officials. It was evident, from the first, that the local authorities were much opposed to the execution of our project, and would try every underhand means in their power to prevent us making the trip. The following will give an instance of the difficulty of dealing with Chinese officials. When it was desired to make a start, no coolies to carry the chairs and baggage were forth coming, and the Governor-General's petty officer stated that he could procure none, as the graduates from the Provincial examination had engaged them all. This appeared to us to be untrue, so General Le Gendre sent the officer away and proceeded to engage the required number himself. This was easily done: a sort of chair-coolie broker, or head man, was called in, and, at once, agreed to supply twenty-five men at $4.50 per head for the trip: one half of the money to be paid in Foochow and the remainder in Amoy. The usual price is $3; but owing to the fact that we were foreigners, an additional $1,50 was asked for and paid.

The Foochow Chinese Board of Trade for the transaction of foreign official affairs. General Le Gendre was so dissatisfied with the conduct of the officials of the Board of Trade, whose duty it was to render every assistance in their power, that he started late in the afternoon to see Ting Chia-wei, one of its principal members. The board of trade is called in Chinese, T'ung-Shang Tsung-Chü (通商總局), or general board of trade; but its duties consist in managing affairs arising out of intercourse with foreigners. The title of Board of Trade, therefore, hardly gives to a foreigner a correct idea of its duties, which are very important. It consists of three members. One having the honorary rank of Provincial Treasurer, the second that of Intendant; the third being the Prefect of the city. These officials are spoken of, collectively, as the Tung-Shang-Chü-Sze-Tao, 通商總局司道. The title of the Treasurer is Pu-cheng-tze (布政司) that of the Intendant, Tao-tao (道台). The title of the third member appears to be omitted in the list. The Board was established, I am told, in 1860, after the Treaty of Tientsin. In other parts of China the Intendant is the person with whom Foreign Consuls have to deal. The names of the present members of the board are, 1st, Yeh Yung-yuen (葉永元); 2nd, Ting Chia-wei (丁嘉瑋); 3rd, Yün Si-ming (尹西銘).

Having arrived at the board of trade, Ting Chia-wei (丁嘉瑋) enquired from General Le Gendre why he would not go comfortably on board a steamer to Amoy instead of going round overland. The General told him that the object in view was to see the country and to be able from personal observation to vouch for the efficiency of the Provincial Government (1). The General further remarked that by treaty stipulation it was the duty of the Board to use every effort to facilitate the departure of the intended travellers, they being officials of a friendly power who had a treaty with China; he also said that in the case of Chinese officials, travelling in America they would be treated with greatest consideration by the United States authorities; that after all, it was useless to place further obstacles on his way; for having the right to go overland to Amoy, and having selected that mode of travelling, he would not go by water; and that if no conveyances could be found he would proceed on foot.

After much talk and banter on both sides, Ting agreed to send out and procure chair coolies, telling the General that he had, however, better borrow chairs for himself and friends, as there were none similar to those employed by foreigners to be had in the city, ready made. This statement proved ultimately to be untrue as the General procured two new ones that evening, without any trouble, through the servants of Baron de Meritens, the hospitable Commissioner of the Imperial Maritime Customs with whom he was staying at the time.

Our adventures now really began. We had arrived at the Board of Trade at about sunset, and after waiting there for upwards of an hour, a messenger came in and informed us that the city gates had been shut, and we were locked within the walls. The Tartar General is custodian of the keys of the gates, which are deposited with him every night after sunset.

(1) Ting Chia-wei understood well that General Le Gendre alluded to the Tientsin Massacre.

So, to his great mortification, Ting was obliged to send a messenger to obtain them. After waiting an hour or nearly so, the messenger returned and told us that the Tartar General, hearing that General Le Gendre was inside of the walls and desired to return to the foreign settlement before morning, had, with pleasure, given orders to open the gates and let us out. We found out afterwards that Baron de Meritens, alarmed at not seeing General Le Gendre return before the closing of the gates, had written to the Tartar General, begging him to render us all possible assistance in case of need. We accordingly left Ting. When we arrived at the gates of the city, we found that the keys had not been sent, and we were obliged to wait sitting in our chairs for another fifteen minutes and soon became the objects round which a crowd of admiring Chinese assembled. They were not rude in the least, however, so that we had nothing much to complain of. The doors having at length been opened we proceeded on our way, and, after an hours rapid walking on the part of our chair coolies, we found ourselves again at the Baron de Meritens, at 8.30 P. M.

First day, January 3rd. Next morning January 3rd at 8 A. M., we left the house of Baron de Meritens, escorted by another staff officer of the Vice-Roy, whom, at the urgent request of Ting, General Le Gendre had allowed to remain in attendance.

Foochow, a city of the first class. As we had to go through the suburbs of Foochow which we could see from the height to the right of the Baron's house, I will give a rapid description of it. Foochow-fu (福 州 府) is situated on the banks of the river Min (閩 江) in the province of Fookien (福 建) of which it is the capital. It is the residence of the Vice-Roy or Tsung-tu (總 督) of Fookien (福 建) and Chekiang (浙 江) and of the other Provincial authorities, the Governor (Fu-tai 撫 台) of Fookien, the General in command of the Tartar garrison (Chiang chun 將 軍) the Provincial Treasurer (Pu-cheng-tze 布 政 司) and the Provincial Judge (An-cha-sze 按 察 司), and it is a Fu (府) or a city of the first class.

Foochow and its suburbs contain about 600,000 inhabitants. The walls are in good repair, and are, I should think, about seven miles in circumference. It contains an Examination Hall where the scholars compete for literary degrees, and, on the south side, it has an enormously long bridge which communicates between two portions of its suburbs. The foreign settlement is at a distance of about three miles outside the walls. In Chinese literary compositions it is sometimes called by its ancient name Yung-chêng (榕城), or Banian city, from the great number of trees of that description that thrive in the city and outside its boundaries. There are three hills within the town, the two principal of which are Woo-shih-shan (烏石山), Black Rock Hill and Chiu-sien-shan (九仙山) the Hill of the nine genii. The British consul has a city residence on Woo-shih-shan.

The country between Foochow & Fang-k'o. Having left Foochow, after passing over a large plain highly cultivated generally, we arrived at a small town or village distant 35 li (12 miles) from the foreign settlement at Foochow. Here we took boats and after proceeding about five miles between the river banks, came to a landing place, and after a short walk, stopped to lunch, at a temple called Fu-hsing-sze (福星寺). The country through which we passed had been all along flat with a back ground of high mountain ranges rising one above the other, at a distance of fifteen or twenty miles, with low spurs of hills running into the plain.

The character of the country appeared to indicate that, under cultivation, it would produce large crops of rice, sugar cane &c.; but during our tour it was under tillage, and we were unable to form from actual observation, an estimate of its grain growing properties (1).

The water communications appeared to be very fine. Late in the afternoon we struck the imperial road, which is about 3 feet wide, paved with slabs of blue and black porphyry, the product of the hills close by. At about 5 o'clock we arrived at a place called Fang-k'o (坊口) and put up for the night. The inn there was small and draughty, and was therefore extremely uncomfortable.

We left at about 7.30 A. M., the next day, 4th January, having breakfasted on hard boiled eggs and claret.

Second day, we leave Fang-k'o. Before leaving Fang-k'o, next day, we were compelled to buy a Chinese umbrella and some oiled paper to protect ourselves and luggage from the wet. Our road led towards the mountains through a fine level country, where we saw a mill worked by water. At

(1) The first day of our trip, we saw the farmers engaged in burning stacks of millet &c. in heaps of earth, as it is done in the manufacture of charcoal, in order, we supposed, to bring out their fertilizing properties. It is very likely then, that, in China, they have known the value of charcoal as a fertilizer, long before us, its use for that purpose being among us, of a recent date.

10 A. M, we crossed a spur of the hills. After a long walk we reached a place called Yang-mei, (陽美), 35 li from Fang-k'o and lunched in a frightfully dirty inn. The weather was extremely cold, and was rather enclined to be wet. At 3.30 the geological aspect of the hills changed, passing from the porphyry to the granite. At 5.30 we arrived at a large village called Yü-chi (漁溪) where we stopped for the night in a Kung-kwan (公館) a sort of residence used by Mandarins when travelling—a sort of official inn, in fact.

During this second day of our trip the scenery, along the road, was very fine, and we passed several monuments to various people: one, in particular, to a great military leader, who, in former years, had preserved the city of Foochow from invasion, and probably destruction. The stone arches of these monuments were generally in ruins, making it evident that the rebels had been in the vicinity at some previous period. We crossed also several small bridges generally with five arches. One had thirteen.

The People are very civil all along the route. Third day, we leave Yu-chi. The people all along the road were very civil and most respectful, rising as we were passing by, to do us honor; and it is very likely that they had received notice of the fact that foreign officials were on a tour through their country. We left Yü-chi, at 8.30 on Thursday morning, 5th January. We walked several miles passing through a long valley and at 11 o'clock came in sight of an arm of the sea, with a number of Junks in the distance. The population about this part of the country appears to consist to a large extent of fishermen. The scenery is very fine, and, as we walked by the high road, we had the sea on our left and high green hills on our right, covered with quantities of pine saplings. At 12.30 we arrived at a place called Chiang-kó (江口) where a small river runs into the arm of the sea. The river is crossed here by a bridge of great length. Half way along the Bridge stands a sort of wooden archway which informs passers by that here the Fuh-ching District (福清縣) separates from the Hsing-hwa (興化).

The old walled town of Chang-ko. On crossing the bridge one enters the old walled town of Chiang-ko (江口). The walls are in a state of great ruin, but the inside of the town does not seem to be in bad repair. We passed directly through it and tiffined at a small Kung-kwan (公館) outside.

Village of Pu-wei. After walking about four miles we came to a small village named Pu-wei (布尾) where we took boats for Hsing-hwa-fu (興化府). We passed on our way through a large village called Han-chiang (涵江) where the canal was so narrow that it barely allowed the boat to pass between its stone embankments. This canal is about thirty-five miles long and was dug only fifty years ago by a General in the Chinese army. There are said to be ninety-nine tributaries to it in its length, and it passes through a rich country.

The walled city of Hsing-hwa-fu. At 7 p. m., we arrived at the walled city of Hsing-hwa-fu (興化府) and slept in the worst inn that we had met with on the trip. Indeed it smelt horribly of everything disgusting.

Hsing-hwa contains a population of about 30,000 inhabitants; but the country round it under the charge of a Prefect is said to have a population of 400,000. The walls are in a good state of preservation and are, I should think, about four miles in circumference.

Fourth day. We left the place at 7.30 a. m., on the 6th of January. The country appeared to be more heavily wooded than hetherto. It is entirely granitic in formation and abounds in quartz veins peeping out of the earth.

We noticed a water mill with an overshot wheel. The appearance of the tombs and monuments show that rebels have been in the neighbourhood. At noon and about forty-three li from Hsing-hwa-fu, we passsed through a small village full of dirty inns, where we took our lunch in a small temple. We now got into a rougher country cut up with dry water courses. The rock appeared to be intirely composed of disintegrated granite. The houses were built of stone and wood and wore a more cleanly appearance than those we had previously seen. We slept at To-ling eighty li from Hsing-hwa.

Fifth day. The walled city of Hwei-gnan-hsien. We left To-ling (土嶺) on Saturday, the 7th of January, at 6.45 a. m., and passed at noon through Hwei-ngan-hsien. (惠安縣), a walled city of the third class, outside which we stopped to tiffin. It has suffered much from the depredations of the population of the surrounding country and the long haired rebels (Chang-mao-tsei 長毛賊). The former have the name of being excessively turbulent. They rose in the 11th year of Hien-Fung (咸豐 1861) and seized the city which they nearly distroyed.

In the first and third year of Tung-chih (同 治), 1863 and 1865, the long haired rebels visited the place and they held it for six months, on the second occasion. The Hsien (縣) magistrate, having led some troops against them, was killed at Lo-yang-chiao (洛 陽 橋). The town does not now contain more than three thousand persons at most.

The town of Lo-yang. Remarkable Bridge. In the afternoon we passed through another town named Lo-yang (洛 陽). There is a bridge which was built about the 10th century by an officer and scholar of the Sung Dynasty, named Tsai-siang (蔡 商). Along its sides stone tablets are erected commemorating its repair by benevolent individuals, and, on a small island, which divides it into two parts, there is an archway with some old inscriptions in it. It has seventy three arches and is about half a mile long.

The Country as we approached Chuen-chow-fu (泉 州 府) has a great number of monuments; and as we crossed a range of hills and from the top of the pass, we could see the walls of the city which are said to be sixteen miles in circumference. They are in good repair.

The walled city of Chuen-chow-fu. Chuen-chow (泉 州) is a place of resort, I am told, for the Literati and retired officials of the Province. Before arriving at the gate by which one enters the city from the high road, there are large numbers of arches and monuments and the Hill sides are completely covered with graves. We went some little distance into the town and put up at 5. P. M. at a large inn, there being no Kungkwan to recieve us. Our small mandarin went to the Yamen of the Prefect to see about one; but came back with a message to the effect that the building, used by the Tartar General and other high dignitaries when travelling was, owing to the long period which had elapsed since the town had been visited, very much out of repair, that the doors and windows had been pulled down and the floors were much broken.

Sixth day. We slept at the inn; and in the morning of sunday, January 8, started at 6.30 with an escort of four soldiers, the authorities were afraid that we might suffer insult. Near the gate through which we left and inside the walls is a large drill ground; and just outside of the city we came upon a bridge about one thousand feet in length crossing the river that enters the sea at Chuen-chow (泉 州).

Contrary to what had been said we found the people on the road most civil. One instant we thought we might suffer some rudness from a body of spearmen, about fifty, I should say, armed with pikes about eighteen feet long; but they passed quietly on their way however, and made room for our chairs. We took our lunch at a place without name and at 4 p. m. we put up at a rather clean inn for the night at Sha-chi (沙溪).

Village of Sha-chi. The distance from Chuen-chow (泉州) to Sha-chi (沙溪) is thirty one miles, and the country is hilly with water ways quite dry.

Seventh day. Town of Low-woo-tien. Town of Amoy. We left our inn, on the 9th January before the sun got well up.. At noon we arrived at Lew-woo-tien (劉五店) a small town at the waters edge, where we took our lunch in the Yamun of a small Mandarin. We left for Amoy Island at 1 o'clock taking a small boat to carry us across. At 2.10 p. m. after a passage of thirty li we landed; and at 5 we arrived at the town of Amoy, whence we crossed over to Ku-lang-seu (鼓浪嶼), the Drum Wave Island, as it is called, where the United States Consulate is situated.

Opinion of Mr. Sibbald as to the influence of the subaltern officers upon the people. There is no doubt that the power of the authorities, if exercised in the right direction, is a great check upon the populace in their conduct towards us. I do not believe either that the natives would attack or insult foreigners were it not that they did so in connivance with their own petty Mandarins and Literati. During our whole journey the only feeling that appeared to influence the people was that of curiosity. They crowded round us at the inns when we stopped at noon or in the evening, and, as we passed along the road, rushed with one accord to gaze at the strange beings who were passing so confidently through their country. We went entirely unarmed; we had not even a revolver with us. In certain places along the route, near the sea shore, the inhabitants have the reputation of being unruly and inclined to rise against the authorities, and there are watch-towers placed half a mile a part, or less in some districts, in which the inhabitants keep watch at night to give the alarm in case of the approach of marauders, the landing of pirates or enemies of any kind. At a regular intervals of ten li (about 3½ miles) there are small guard houses with three short chimneys either beside or in front of them in which in case of a rising, fires would be lighted in order that the smoke assending might alarm the soldiers in the next military station; but on our whole trip we did not see a soldier either in, or in the vicinity of one of the guard houses (1). Neither did we meet any constabulary or police force to assist the authorities in the maintainance of order. We saw one robber or murderer being carried to Foochow in a wooden cage. We could not find out with certainly what his crime was, but it was evidently one to be punished with death; and he was in the charge of two policemen unarmed!

Foochow, 11th February, 1871.

(Signed) W. LEE SIBBALD.

My views of the government of the middle Empire. To understand this state of affair, so different from that for which late accounts of China had prepared us, one is required to have lived in the East or to have devoted sometime to the study of the social and political organisation of the people there. What distinguishes the Chinese from Western races and renders the task of their rulers easier is that they have, I believe, a different idea of Society than we have ourselves, in this, that while we always think of the rights which we have acquired in gathering together as a nation, and are very apt to loose sight of the obligations which we have contracted thereby, the reverse is the case with them; and to teach children those duties which will be binding upon them as men, is almost the exclusive task of those who, in China, are intrusted with public training.

To this end the whole System of Government is based upon patriarchal authority, and filial pety is the sentiment which is first inculcated in man's heart, the other virtues being considered as subsidiary to it. The authority of the father and of the mother is absolute. It takes advice from nobody and it ows account of its decisions to no one. It includes

---

(1) The Governor General of Fookien gives an explanation of this state of affairs in his secret memorial to the Emperor, part of which I have quoted in Memorandum No. 2; he says: "Of late we have not kept any permanent army in Fookien for the defence of the Ports. The Provincial Treasury has been so much impoverished by the unusual expense of the 3rd year of this reign that we have been compelled to disband the regular force sent from the province of Hounan and Houpei, to aid us in putting down the rebellion and now we have but the number of Soldiers which is strictly required for the maintainance of order."

the right of life and death which the Emperor himself never exercises, but when called upon to confirm, with the approval of the Censors, the decision of the tribunals.

How excessive this right of parents may seem it has nevertheless proved beneficial, natural feelings, doubtless being an effective safeguard against the abuses which may result from it; and, besides, parents seldom live alone with their children; a common roof often shelters three or four generations with their different branches and the impulsiveness of the young one must be tempered down by the authority of the elder people when this has not already been accomplished by their example. In this way paternal supervision whereby a watchful eye is always kept on the family, foreseeing its wants, unwrapping its thoughts and opposing its faults, constitutes the most powerful auxiliary which a government such as that existing in China, could possibly have to its action, and keeps it always amply provided with a healthful supply of subjects long prepared for submission.

I could not better compare Chinese families than to a company of soldiers which is, as we know, the lowest unit of military organisation.˙ In it all are hierarchically arranged and being submissive to their respective chiefs, as soldiers, in camps, are to their petty officers and to their higher commanders. This life in common, somewhat like that which Fourier had dreamed for his Phalanstery, offers the advantage which must be very great in a crowded country like China, to be very economical. And, in return, it has very few inconveniences, for, in spite of the collection of so many persons within such narrow limits, good health is general, at the least in the country, doubtless owing to the peculiar way the Chinese have of building their houses which enables them to live almost constantly in open air and to the fulness of their dress which aids the free circulation of the blood and is calculated to easily adapt itself not only to season, but also to sudden changes of temperature.

None except military and naval men can officiate in the Province of their birth or where they have married, that they may be kept away from influences foreign to the general good. The Prefects who are instrusted more especially with the police and the administration of justice and the collection of the land taxes, are called the fathers of the people, being *de facto* the senior *pater familias* of their districts. At the door of each house may be seen, written on a board or on slips of paper, the names and the ages of the members of the family, servants or slaves, should there be any, included.

There are distant places which remain outside of the immediate jurisdiction of the regular authority, they being without importance and the taxes which could be collected therein not being judged sufficient to cover the expenses connected with the establishment of an imperial office. In such cases the people appoint a head man whom they pay and keep in office as long as they are satisfied with his administration. Although without acknowledged rank, many of those head men are known to have at their command a regular force of soldiers, which they use in enforcing the local laws and in repressing desorder, and, in this, they are supported by the Imperial Authorities who acknowledge them as the representatives of the people and transact all their business of the District with them. And thus Democracy is found to exist in its purest form in perhaps the most despotic country on the face of the earth.

Primitive as it is, this system of Goveramnent adapts itself better to the Chinese, I believe, than anything which we may offer as a substitute; and to strenghten their Government and to enable it as much as possible to exert its authority over its distant possessions, we only stand in the way by insisting upon them conforming to us, and in this lies, in a great measure, the secret of the failure of the foreign policy in China for twelve years past. Confident of the future and, in the magnitude of our strength, we should avoid asking for any blunt change and be satisfied with such reforms as would compel the officers in the provinces to conform to their antique laws causing the same to be modified from time to time and little by little, that they may be better calculated to assist into the carrying out of the existing treaties, meet the requirements of the age, and aid to, instead of obstructing, as they often do, the improvement of the relations both social and commercial which must exist between these two races. Once the Empire fairly open, Religion and Civilization must soon follow on the track open by trade.

The Pekin Mission. To witness this gigantic struggle between the East and the West, to aid in the accomplishment of the work of transformation which must be the result of it, the best men should be selected on both sides. As for America she needs at Peking her ablest statesmen, men of the highest order, men of calibre and experience, men that will be above all petty influences or interests, men that will despise coming before the world with temporary or fictitions triumphs, men of energetic character, broad views and sound morals. There is for such men a great career open in the East for fifty years to come, a career as great as ever there was at home for any one. For China is nearer to us than she is to any other manufacturing countries. She contains 360,000,000 inhabitants, and when we have attained our highest degree of industrial and agricultural development and therefore, will be able to offer to the world the necessaries which are now derived solely from the Continent of Europe, the relations between her and ourselves, as guaranteed by the necessities of both nations, must receive an impulse the measure of which no one can foretell; and if the object in view of the Minister we have in Peking must be to secure us an influence with the Chinese that will guarantee us in the future a share of such a trade, we may, without further comments, realize the extent of the services that a man of genius, in that position, may render to his country.

Amoy, 25th April, 1871.

MEMORANDUM No. 4.

THE DISTURBANCES IN THE AMOY DISTRICT
PREVIOUS TO THE MASSACRE OF TIENTSIN, AND HOW THEY WERE DEALT WITH.

Memorandum No. 4.

THE DISTURBANCES IN THE AMOY DISTRICT PREVIOUS TO THE MASSACRE OF TIENTSIN, AND HOW THEY WERE DEALT WITH.

Sine irá and Studio.
Tacitus.

Why this paper is submitted. If the views which I have submitted upon subjects of public concern in China, had always met with general approval, I would not fatigue you with the narrative of events which are now forgotten and, practically and in themselves, have ceased to be of any interest to the people.—But, indeed, as, in connection with these occurrences, I have been at variance with my superiors, in Peking, chiefly regarding the construction to be placed upon the instructions of the home office in what relate to the appeal which it is contemplated Consuls may have to make to the navy for assistance, a subject, you will concede, fully deserving our attention, now that, at any time, we may be called upon to act in defence of our countrymen in these distant lands, I have thought well to the extend further with these notes.

The year 1868 was an eventful one with us. The warning for the storm came from central Formosa; but the first outbreack took place in the northern portion of that Island.

The Banca difficulties. On the 13th of October the Vice-Consul for England received a communication from Mr. Kerr, managing partner of a British firm established at Banca, reporting that a most cruel outrage had been perpetrated, on the previous day, at that place, on himself and on Mr. Bird, a clerk in the house. On receipt of the news, I crossed over in the U. S. Gun-boat *Aroostook* under command of Captain Bradford, for the purpose of watching American interests which I had good reasons to believe were threatened, Mr. Kerr, upon whom the assault had been made, at the time, being acting Commercial Agent for us. I arrived in Tamsui in the afternoon of the 24th.

During the evening, I received the visit from the Ting (District magistrate) who informed me that, through his exertions, order had been restored in the town of Banca, of which the small hamlet of Howei is the Port. However he did not conceal his fears that it could not be maintained if the British Gun-boat *Janus*, then at anchor in the Port, should go further up the river; and therefore, he begged me to call the attention of H. B. M.'s Consul on the subject. I, at first, refused to be mixed up with an affair that I did not consider to be within my province. Mr. Kerr was a British subject; he had not been assaulted while performing any official duties for the United States. Americans had not been molested by the mob; they were at liberty to pursue their business, at all hours of the day, in the town of the Port; what right had I then to interfere? The Ting, appreciating my scruples, retired.

On the 25th Captain Bradford called upon the Ting, and stated to him that he endorsed my views. On the same day I returned the call of the Ting, and, during my visit, he submitted to me a Despatch from Mr. Consul Holt, stating that the demands, therein, were ellegal and that he could not acquiesce to them.

<small>Mr. Holt's demands.</small> Mr. Holt's Despatch concluded as follows: "I therefore now demand: I. An apology to be offered to me from the Tamsuy Ting for the affront offered to me on the morning of the 12th of October, in his office at Banca."

II. "The punishment of the Hwang-clan, and of the head-men named in the margin."

III. "That for the serious injuries on Messrs. Kerr and Bird, for the entire stoppage of their trade, and for the loss of prestige which they have sustained, the local authorities shall compel from the Hwang-clan a payment of $5,000, to be made to Messrs. Dodd & Co."

IV. "The issue by the Tamsuy Ting of a proclamation, denouncing the late assault on Messrs. Kerr and Bird, to be cut in a stone tablet, ordering the people to pay every respect to foreign merchants trading in Banca, and within the Tamsuy District, and threatening severe punishment in the event of their being molested."

V. "That all the personal property stolen on the occasion of the assault, be returned or amply compentated for."

VI. "That the authorities shall use their utmost diligence in arresting as many of the assailants of Messrs. Kerr and Bird as they can, and that they shall all be severely punished and imprisoned."

VII. "That both their old hong and the Loktow hong shall be restored to Messrs. Dodd & Co. without delay, and full compensation made for such goods as may be missing."

VIII. "That on the day on which the authorities notify that the Loktow hong is ready to be delievered over to Messrs. Dodd & Co., the Tamsuy Ting, the Commander of the man of war, with his guard and myself, accompanied by Messrs. Kerr and Bird, with twelve of the principal leaders of the late assault, in heavy cangues, shall proceed to the said hong, through the same streets which they were driven through; and that the said hong shall be formally delivered over to them; and the twelve men be kept in cangues in front of the said hong, for one month from the date of entry under a guard of soldiers."

IX. "That a guard of soldiers be stationed at Banca, to prevent Messrs. Dodd & Co.'s agents being again assaulted."

"If these conditions are not fulfilled precisely by 10 o'clock, in the morning of the 27th instant, I shall, at once, be compelled to take other measures." I have &c., &c. (signed) Henry F. Holt.

Having fully examined the document, I advised the Ting to send a verbal reply, which I agreed to unofficially offer, in his name, to H. B. M.'s Consul.

Mr. Holt assents to the Ting's views of the case. Therefore, on the 25th, in the evening, I begged from H. B. M.'s Consul privilege to submit the Ting's views, in which, after a short discussion, Mr. Holt concurred; and, on the 26th, with the consent and knowledge of the Consul, I held communication with the local authorities, who agreed to abide to seven rules prepared by me and embodying these views. They were as follows:—

RULE I.—The Tamsuy Ting shall, this day, address a Despatch to the Hai-kwan, stating that the affront, offered at Banca to the Vice-Consul's card, has been punished by the dismissal of the offending servants; and that, had the Tamsuy Ting being present in Banca, at the time, the servants would never have dared to use such words, or to act as they did.

RULE II.—The assault on Messrs. Kerr and Bird by the Hwang-clan, was decidedly wrong. Four of the principal ring leaders have been taken and punished, and, during the space of one month, from this date, will be kept in cangues in front of the Tamsuy Ting's office.

RULE III.—The Tamsuy Ting will issue a proclamation, instructing the people to be on friendly terms with foreigners and to conduct their business with them amicably. Three copies will be issued to-morrow; one to be given to Messrs. Dodd & Co., which they may cause to be cut in stone, one to be put up in the public streets, and the third to be delivered to Mr. Holt, H. M.'s Acting Vice-Consul.

RULE IV.—Hwang-chang-she (man soon) had no right to the property in dispute; and in taking it upon herself to lease it without the necessary regard for the opinions and desires of her relatives, has committed a grave fault, for which she must pay a fine of $3,000 within the next month, His Excellency the Hai-kwan guaranteeing the amount.

RULE V.—Messrs. Dodd & Co. are requested to send in an account for certain pieces of goods, &c., which were lost during the time of the assault and since that period, in order that the value may be made good to them.

RULE VI.—For the assault on Messrs. Kerr and Brid, the Hwang-clan has been fined $1,000 Dollars.

RULE VII.—At Banca, there are only police runners; it is therefore necessary to inform the heads of the people that they must exercise their authority on the people of their respective wards, and must cause friendly relations to be entertained towards foreigners. Supposing any troubles occasionally arise, the matter must be immediately reported to the Tamsuy Ting's office, in order that the matter may be impartially investigated by him, in conjunction with the Vice-Consul; a copy of the Bond to be entered into by the head man shall be sent to the Vice-Cousul.

Final Settlement of the affair. In the afternoon I left for Banca where I spent the night. Early in the morning, of the 28th, the Ting held his court and, at 10 o'clock, when I left, the stipulations agreed upon had been fully carried out:—The guilty parties had been placed in heavy cangues; the security promised had been given; all the fines had been paid; the Chinese agents of Mssrs. Dodd & Co. were freely pursuing their occupations in their hong. On my way back to my boat I was received with unmistakable marks of respect by the population of the town. I reached the Port of the town of Banca at 2 o'clock. I visited H. B. M.'s Consul the same evening, when he had the kindness to hand me a letter of thanks. Early next morning we left the Port, and on the 24th, in the morning, we were at anchor in Amoy.

The settlement is approved by H. B. M.'s Minister, by the Vice-Roy of Fookien & Chekiang & by the Earl of Clarendon. A few months after, H. B. M.'s Minister tendered thanks to Lieutenant Commander Bradford and myself officially through the Ambassador of the United States for what he was pleased to call the moral support we had given to Mr. Holt, at Banca. The Vice-Roy of Fookien and Chekiang, himself, did not delay in informing me of the pleasure caused to him by the adjustment of the affair; and, finally, the Earl of Clarendon instructed Sir R. Alcock to inform Mr. Holt that Her Majesty's Government approved of his conduct in this matter.

My conclusions. To the great wisdom of the Ting, to his unmistakable firmness, and to the rare conciliatory spirit exhibited by Mr. Holt, is due the peaceful adjustment of this difficulty which might have been, in the Tamsuy district, the cause of a bloody contest, of serious embarrassments to the Chinese, and of great injury to foreign trade—and for the sake of the hint which I thought this settlement, as brought on by us, might be to all in future occurrences, I had thus allowed myself to be brought in between the contending parties. All this labor was not, however, productive of the results which I had expected. On my return to Amoy I heard that Liang Tautai, the Governor of Formosa, seeing himself relieved from the embarrassment which he had once feared the Banca affair would cause for him, with and by the advice of the Vice Roy of the Province, had issued orders to treat foreigners, in central Formosa, with renewed vigor.

Judging from their past aggressive attitude, not only in the Island and on the main, but almost everywhere in the Empire, we had just causes for apprehension as to our safety.

Review of events in central Formosa since the month of May previous. We were in November, and already, in central Formosa, Messrs. Elles & Co.'s Camphor had been most unjustly confiscated; their Comprador's house had been plundered and made a mass of ruins. He himself had been seized and thrown into prison, his only crime being his connexion with a foreign firm. On the 25th of June following, the community was startled at receiving the intelligence that the Intendant had sent a force against Mr. Pickering and had set a price on his head. Afterwards, on the 3rd of July, Mr. Hardy, of Messrs. Tait & Co., was stabbed in a public street, in the middle of the day, in a village near Takao; but the would be assassin was allowed to escape, nor was any effort made to seize him. The most outrageous reports on a Dr. Maxwell, through whose desinterested exertions, thousands of Chinese had been ta'::en from the grasp of death, were spread about with a view to excite the ignorant multitude against him, and this simply because, to a work inherent to a medical man, he added that of a preacher of the gospel. His life was several times threatened, and finally his house was burned down (31st of October). We remember that Mr. Kerr had been attacked in the northern portion of the Island, during the first part of the same month.

The catholic priests were not better treated; their mission being twice burned down. Previous to this, the foreign settlements at Takao had been several times threatened by the mob, the Tau-tai always refusing to listen to the complaints of the Consuls. During the May previous, being in Takao myself, I was a witness to this criminal indifference on his part. Large bands of banditti were reported to be marching on the settlement from the south. Troops were sent for, but were refused by the Intendant Liang; and although Chêntai Lew, the military commander of the Island, was willing to call out the militia, Liang or his subordinates refused to supply him with the necessary funds. In this predicament, the community and the British Consul called through me upon captain Beardslee, U. S. N., then in port, for assistance. A spot where guns, the property of Messrs. Elles & Co., should be placed in position was selected by me, at the request of captain Beardslee, who agreed to supply the necessary ammunition from his ship; and the mob, hearing of our preparations, soon retired. Subsequently the authorities were simply asked to issue a proclamation; but even this they neglected to do; for, if indeed the proclamation was written, it was never posted.

Mr. Jameson who had remained in charge of the British Consulate during all this time was soon succeeded by Mr. Gibson; but, instead of improving, things went from bad to worse. With a view to avoid the annoyances of personal interviews or of correspondence, the Intendant added insult to injury. He refused to recognize the Consul.

On the 17th of August, at a meeting of the Citizens of all nations, resolutions were passed, urging the necessity of calling upon the navy for protection. They represented that a large force was required, observing with great wisdom, that a small display would only exasperate the populations already excited by their rulers; and, until such force would come, they determined to leave Taiwanfoo and go to the subsidiary Port of Takao, where, from the peculiar topography of the country, they may hope more successfully to defend themselves.

From that time, 17th of August, until Anping was taken, 20th of November, no foreigners visited Taiwanfoo or left any of their property within its walls. All trade was suspended.

When it came to this, Mr. Gibson had, I conceive, to call upon the navy, not to use force, but to lend him the moral support of its presence. He only requested the senior naval officer at Hongkong to furnish him with a gunboat for defensive purpose.

On the 26th of August, Lord Charles Scott determined to proceed to Takao, I can safely say, for he told me so, with a view to bring about an amicable settlement of the disputes. Hearing that I was on the spot when the difficulties originated, knowing that I had been mixed in them through the joint action of the Chinese and of H. B. M.'s Consul, when the first complications took place, with a rare courtesy, he came to the Consulate, to consult on the theory of the case, and inquire whether the presence of his forces before Taiwanfoo would enterfere with my plans of adjustment of the camphor question. I gave him copies of my despatches to the Vice-Roy on the subject, and he left with the "Rinaldo," having also the "Dwarf under his orders." Having arrived in Anping he investigated the whole case, weighing carefully the causes of complaint. He left fully satisfied that nothing but force would bring the Tautai to terms. However both he and Mr. Gibson, judging that they had not sufficient authority to act, or enough force to insure success, if they did, they reported for orders to their respective superiors.

On the 26th of September, Mr. Gibson wrote to the Minister:—"I shall wait until Your Excellency send me instructions as to my future proceedings, but perhaps circumstances will not permit me to wait. If unforeseen circumstances will not permit this, I shall act with great caution, following out every link in the chain of success that binds foreign trade and Missionary enterprize to Formosa, well assured of your Excellency's sympathy and approval." By Dispatch, dated October 24th, Sir Rutherford approved of all Mr. Gibson's correspondence up to the 27th of September. He doubtless then judged the situation of affairs precarious in Formosa, for he wrote of it to the Admiral; and Sir H. Keppel who previously had received a report from Lord Scott, came to Amoy to complete in a personal interview with his subordinate, whatever written information he had received from him on the subject. He wrote to the Minister (10th of December): That it was specially requisite to convince the authorities of the British abilities to enforce a due respect for the treaty rights; that he disaproved of coercive threats being employed without ample'means being at hand to carry them out.

Preparations made by the Admiral to enforce the treaties in Central Formosa. To provide such means he had directed Captain Ross to proceed to Formosa in the *Pearl*, where he would take the *Perseus*, the *Rinaldo*, and *Dwarf* and four others under his orders. He said also that he thought that the first of his operations would probably be the capture and occupation of Anping and Taiwanfoo, and he had therefore instructed the Senior Naval officer on the Coast of Formosa to act in accordance with these views and he hoped to reach Shanghai in January where the Rodney awaited him, and he should be in position to join the force off Takao a few days later, should circumstances demand his presence. The Senior officer at Takao had been instructed to act in concurrence with the Consul to whom he was to afford a cordial support and effective force.

The Vice-Roy of Foochow sends a Commissioner to Central Formosa. While all this was going on and while the resort to force was judged necessary both by the British Minister and by the Admiral, although Mr. Gibson knew nothing of those despatches having passed through, the Imperial Commissioner Tseng was directed by the Vice-Roy of the Province to proceed to Taiwanfoo.

Tseng Taotai most reluctantly accepted the mission tendered to him; and even after he had accepted it he made all sorts of excuses not to go; and he left only on receipt of a most peremptory order of the Vice-Roy, at once to embark and to proceed to Taiwan and not leave the ship until he had reached his destination. I had just returned from Northern Formosa, (31st October)—and I heard that he was most anxious to see me. But being confined to his ship, lying at anchor in the Amoy harbor, under pretext of stormy weather outside, he sent to me an officer on the staff of Admiral Lee, with a verbal message, begging me to come. And, as I delayed, he wrote me a private note. Seeing his distress, I, at once, complied with his request, and handed over to him a paper, which he had asked me to prepare, giving my views of the difficulties which had arisen in central Formosa. I had been careful to submit the paper to my colleagues who, without exception, safe the Consul for Spain, had assented to it. Tseng-Tayen read it with the greatest attention, and when he had finished he said that the case was so complicated that he should like me to accompany him to Formosa and assist him with the British and the French Consul whom he dreaded much to have dealings with, not having met them before, and he knew they were my friends. I replied that I would gladly go, provided I could settle my affairs in the two days he offered to wait for me in the Port of Amoy. But, at the last moment, I concluded to remain, having found out from outside parties that he had not said the truth to me as regards to his commission and that, although in fact he was vested with all the authority of his superior the Governor-General, he had orders not to make use of it, but as a last resort, and, if possible, to limit his action to the investigation of the alleged errors and wrongs of the local Government, and simply to report upon the same that his provincial masters might shift the responsibility of settlement and throw it upon the Tseng-lee Yâmen at Peking for whose interference in the matter they had no thanks to offer.

Tseng Tautai was fully adequate to the task before him; and doubtless he left Amoy having made up his mind to endorse the views of the Governor General in approving the acts of Liang and reporting upon the grievances of foreigners as being futile and of no importance and then return to the mainland leaving both parties to arrange as well as they could, and intending to show after that the conflict which, he knew must take place between the Chinese authorities of Formosa and the British naval officer, had been all brought on by foreigners who, with evil motives, had forced a quarrel upon the Chinese. I was so convinced that this would be the case that I wrote of it to Mr. Gibson, that he might be on his guard.

Tseng, having notified **Mr. Gibson** of his arrival at Tai-wan-foo, the latter lost no time in placing himself in communication with him; and he wrote him a lengthly Despatch in which, having enumerated the crimes and wrongs of Liang Tautai and his subordinates, he submitted the conditions which he felt bound to request from the local Government of Taiwan. This despatch ended as follows:

<small>Mr. Gibson places himself in communication with Tseng Tautai.</small>

"Now I demand, in the name of every principle of justice, that these three officers, viz. Liang Tau-tai, Lin-Lee, the District Magistrate of Fung-shan, and Kew, the Loo-Kiang Ting, be dismissed with disgrace. * * * * * * ; that the accusers of Dr. Maxwell and Kao-chang be tried, and, if found guilty, be most severely punished before a person appointed by me. * * * * * . That Hwang-king and others, if found guilty, should suffer death; and their abettors should be severely punished before a person appointed by me." * * * * *

"That $6,000 be paid within the space of twenty-four hours as indemnity for the camphor officially and illegally removed from Messrs. Elles & Co.'s hired house at Wu-chai, or $6,000 worth of camphor be restored to Messrs. Elles & Co."

"That $1,167 be paid within the space of twenty-four hours to Dr. Maxwell as indemnity for the destruction of the mission property."

"That $2,000 be paid within the space of twenty-four hours as indemnity to catholic fathers for the destruction of their property."

"That Messrs. Elles & Co.'s compradore have his property returned as it was before his house was broken into, or damage given him within the space of twenty-four hours to the exact amount of money and other property removed."

"That a suitable number (say 25) of Proclamations be issued embodying t e first paragraph of the IX article, the whole of the XIII, and the whole of the XIV (of the Treaty). That these Proclamations should guarrantee to British merchants travelling under passports, which passports are to be countersigned by the Tautai and respected, and the Chinese agents of British merchants, liberty to trade in camphor both in the interior of this Island and at coast ports forbidden to foreign vessels, and that these Proclamations should abolish any notifications issued hetherto ordering natives, under the most severe punishments, viz: death, not to sell camphor to foreign merchants."

"That a suitable number (say 25) of proclamations be issued in favor of the Christian religion, Protestant and Catholic, embodying the VIII Article of the Treaty; these Proclamations to involve that the poisonous or noxious drugs which idle reports states that the Missionaries used, is but a piece of mendacious gossip, that the authorities will very severely punish any person who utters such lying affirmations, and that converted natives, not offending against the Laws, are not be persecuted or interfered with.

"That a suitable number (say 10) of Proclamations be issued, embodying the XVII Article of the Treaty, and stating that whenever such cases arisen between a British subject or their Agents, and a Chinese subject, as that the Consul cannot settle them amicably, he shall request the assistance of the Chinese authorities and that these authorities shall come.

"All these conditions are fair and just. Liang Tautai and his subordinates simply laugh at them. I think you, as an honest, intelligent and straight-forward officer, will very much regret their procedure and I request you to report the gross malfeasance of the local Government.

"I shall conclude by four remarks: "I have written this Despatch to you, and will show you all the documents that I have in my possession upon this subject, simply for your information; but you have come over here with very defective powers, utterly incapable of suspending, even for a moment, the Tautai or any other officers's Commission. It was on account of your defective powers that I refused to discuss with you subsidiary affairs; not on account of your requiring proof of Liang Tautai's misdeeds. Your desiring evidence of those wrongs of which I accuse Liang Tautai, I consider as very fair and impartial; and I beg to submit this Despatch, the office Despatches, and a host of witnesses, as indisputable proof. * * * * * *

"The wrongs inflicted by Liang Tantai on British subjects are of eight or nine months duration. I have been very patient under these afflictions; but those proceedings must come to an end very shortly; can you not, on your own responsibility, suspend Liang's Commission?

"I must inform you of one error that you made in our conference yesterday. You seemed to assert that British subjects are involved in quarrels with the people generally. *Nothing could be farther from the fact.* British subjects have no complaints to make against the people generally;

but they have loud complaints to make against Liang Tautai and the rest of the officials, their servants, their soldiers, their militia and their hangers on." (Signed) John Gibson.

Mr. Gibson's demands. As I had foreseen, Tseng made light of the Consul's letter, and, with a view to discourage all investigation, he informed Mr. Gibson, before witnesses, Dr. Manson, Mr. Hardy, Lieut. Gordon, Lieut. Johnson and Mr. Taylor, who had been summoned by the Consul, should Commissioner Tseng require evidence from them in the cases in litigation, that he was sent only, " To inquire and report; that the week he had spent in the capital of the Island and its immediate vicinity " (he had come on the 8th and did not see the Consul in Takao till the 16th—during all that time living with the officers against whom charges had been made)—" had been sufficient for his investigation; that, on the 17th, if the British Consul would not settle the two or three cases of indemnity with him, which he considered of very little moment, he would return to Amoy in his steamer, lying in the harbour, on the 18th or 19th.

The position in which Mr. Gibson's was left by Tseng reply considered. Knowing all he knew, when Mr. Gibson saw Tseng taking such a position, what was he to do? He had already broken off all intercourse with Liang Tautai, and stood on the defensive for five months? Two methods of procedure were open to him: 1st, to take a reprisal in order to make Tseng show his real powers, or, 2nd, to call on Europeans under his jurisdiction, to go on board ship and set sail along with Tseng for Amoy.

Mr. Gibson decides for the first alternative. Mr. Gibson, after much consideration, and consultation with the best men in the place decided for the first alternative. And in this, I believe, he acted wisely. For it must be borne in mind that in a country peopled by a race which, when incited by their rulers, is apt to show a degree of barbarism which, seldom has been equalled in the darkest days of the middle ages, "governed by officials who, in certain things, are so little above a state of barbarism themselves, that they had no scruple in placing an ambuscade of armed men to intercept and kill a Consul and naval officer proceeding to the Magistrate's place of residence, on a peaceful mission, and thought the best mode of preventing a merchant from recovering property of which he had been despoiled, was to send people to shoot him down, or to forbit the people under the penalty of death to give him shelter or food. There is enough in such conditions to demoralize all diplomacy, if not to justify a resort to reprisals and acts of hostility not contemplated by Vatel. Mr. Gibson concluded the time had come when it was imperative to give check to an adversary of this stamp by alarming him for his own security, as the only means of paralizing his power of inflicting irreparable injury, and securing from an attack a community not otherwise to be protected; and he determined to take military possession of the fort of Zelandia, and the ramparts of the village of Anping," (1) not only as a material guarantee, in the shape of a reprisal, but as a basis of action, Anping being the key to the capital of Taiwan. He applied to Lt. Gordon, Her Majesty senior naval officer, who approved of his plan of proceedings. Mr. Gibson and Lt. Gordon were off Fort of Zelandia on the 20th. They landed about 3 o'clock P. M. on the same day, and they reconnoitred the fort and the ramparts of the village. They found the doors on the magazines in the fort locked and, from information which Mr. Gibson received, the soldiers and their commandant had all removed. The reconnoitring party took military possession of the fort and the ramparts of the village without opposition. The Consul requested verbally Her Magesty's senior naval officer not to interfere with the civil government of the village, to allow the native merchants to trade as usual, and to protert the foreign Custom House. He posted proclamations over the village of Anping, enjoining the people not to leave home, but to proceed with their different occupations as hitherto; and he transmitted another set of proclamations to Tai-wanfoo, announcing to the inhabitants that, if they molested Her Magesty's Consulate, or the foreign houses, the city should be bombarded. Finally, it was agreed between the Consul and the naval officer that the fort and the ramparts of the village should be held from the ship.

Objections made, in principle, to the act of Mr. Gibson; reply in justification of the same.
"No doubt it was an act of aggression and of war to seize a fort however strictly it may have been intended as a purely defensive measure on the principle that a home thrust is often the best parry. But in dealing with an Eastern race and officials, it will sometimes happen that a few foreigners may be menaced with attack from overwhelming numbers, or under circumstances of disadvantages which would make effective defence impossible. This is a fatal condition which no sane man, if he clearly

(1) Sir R. Alcock to the Lord of Clarendon (unpublished official correspondence.)

foresees it, will voluntary accept it. In such circumstances there may be only one alternative, and that is to strike at your enemy first, where he least expects it or where he may be most vulnerable. In this case flight on board the gunboats was impossible for want of accommodation for the number requiring shelter, and of sufficient means to protest the property of the people." (1)

For it must be remembered that at Takao, which is virtually the Port of Taiwanfoo and where foreigners mostly reside, the wealth of the place is all, i. e. centred in the foreign houses, the Chinese property being merely a few fishermen's huts. And it is likely that if Tseng had left Takao, as announced by him, without making an investigation, Liang-encouraged by impunity, would have found more than one, among his numerous followers, to apply a discreet torch to our settlements. And, in the record of Chinese treachery we have abundant reason to believe that this would have likely been done. When in Taiwanfoo, in 1842, they resolved to murder 197 cast aways, they now say, as a reprisal for the capture of Amoy, they did not send an armed force to overwhelm them. Under the most humain pretext, they divided the infortunate into small parties, and, then, in the dark, during their sleep, they covered them with chains, beheaded them on the public place of execution in Taiwanfoo, leaving their bones without sepulture,—an easy prey for the dogs and kites There are Chinese, now living, that can yet tell the infamous tale. Or in the case of Burgevine, a great criminal in law, may be, but yet a man who, under the treaties, if liable to be sentenced to death, had a right to an American rope: they bribed his servant, a colored man, whom I have seen since in Amoy, and who led him defenceless to their lines. They put him in a boat ostensibly to bring him to Shanghai, caused it to be upset, and the infortunate man, loaded with chains (he had been suffering acute dysentery for many days, and was never once unbound by his captors), sunk deep into the waves, and none remained to relate his fate. I could multiply the instances.

It cannot be contended that in such cases, when danger is imminent, although not immediate, and there are just causes for reprisal, the property should be abandoned, and for its loss, the owners be expected to apply afterwards for indemnification by the Central Government. For who could

---

(1) Sir R. Alcock to the Lord of Clarendon (unpublished official correspondence.)

indemnify them for, or who could estimate the numberless losses contingent on the violent suspension of any business? Further, if it was not in the spirit of the instructions that redress should only be insured against ultimate ruin, why is the contrary stated? and why is it admitted that, in cases of very peculiar nature, a recourse to arms is justifiable?

"If the only remedy when foreign life and property is in danger, is to be flight, if foreign merchants are to be compelled to abandon everything and run away, even such a flight were possible, and no resistance to be made at all to oppression of any sort, I am bound to say my conviction is strong that no foreigners will be allowed to remain long in China. Let the Chinese authorities and Government once know that such is the policy to be pursued by Foreign Powers in every port, they will very soon render our position in Chian untenable. As one of the American Ministers in China once said: "Then indeed the policy of peace will produce no peace." Or at least the peace will be all on one side and only to be attained by the absence of all foreign commerce from the coast of China" (1).

Having carefully considered all this, Mr. Consul Gibson came to the conclusion that this was precisely one of the emergencies where a Consul must take all responsibility to avert a catastrophe which would have proved an irreparable injury to the interests it was his duty to protect at all hazards, and he resolved to take a reprisal which would be a sure means of convincing Tseng that he could not decline acting under his mandate, with impunity, and a reprisal which did not injure trade or be a stumbling block and offence to the people, but fall upon the investigators of the whole course of illegalities, wrongs, and crimes. In such emergencies I should think, a Consul, in a country like China, rises at once to a higher station; he must take the responsibility devolving upon the Minister himself, nay, upon the Government at home and act as the highest authority on the land would have acted had it been on the spot.

The question to decide, therefore, is not to determine whether Mr. Gibson exceeded his powers but whether he made good use of them. For if it is once admitted that it was his duty to protect the people in their lives and property, at all hazards, it must be conceded also that he could not have too great powers. What could Mr. Gibson have done

(1) Sir R. Alcock to the Lord of Clarendon (Unpublished official correspondence).

in this particular case? Blockade the port? There is no port in Taiwanfoo. Stop the junk trade as Sir Rutherford did many years ago in Shanghai? There were no junks in sight. He did the only thing he could, he seized Anping which he had good reasons to believe could be taken possession without effusion of blood.

Parties whose opinion has considerable weight in China, referring to the Yang-chow crisis, where a display of force proved sufficient to secure justice to foreigners, have expressed the regret that the urgent requisition of Her Majesty's Consul at Formosa should have required an act of war when the end could have been gained by a milder form of coercion. I cannot concur in these views. The protracted correspondence resulting from the course of wrongs which I have exposed above, had proved that diplomacy had almost exhausted every effort to bring about a settlement of just claims. And I have it on undoubted authority that Liang said to a foreign Commissioner of Customs, Mr. Kopsh, that he did not care what foreigners might threaten to do, as he would defy them from Taiwanfoo, where no European guns could reach him from the sea, in which delusion he was confirmed by the foreign residents taking refuge in Takao. Therefore, there is very little doubt left in my mind that a display of force would have resulted simply in the force being used. And as the British Admiral had detached eight ships with about six hundred men, who actually came after, this officer, most likely, would have landed his forces and; I know it from reliable source, overrun Formosa, destroying peace which soon after was reestablished upon treaty basis, and he would have annhilated trade and lighted up the flames of rebellion in the Island, for which the natives are always ready.

Tseng resumes the negociations after the occupation of Anping, on the 24d. The understanding he arrive at with Mr. Gibson.

Having heard of what had been done at Anping, on the 23rd, Tseng called at the British Consulate, for an interview, on the 24th, this time not as a simple Deputy but as a Commissioner vested with full powers; and he came to the following understanding with Mr. Gibson. It was agreed between both gentlemen: on the one part, that, as a guarantee of the promises made before to Lord Chs. Scott, in September, and afterwards ignored, the British forces should hold Anping till all Mr. Gibson's conditions were fulfilled. That Mr. Gibson, at once, should notify the naval officer of the agreement made during the day. On the other side, that Tseng would notify this same agreement to the Taiwan Authorities.

Mr. Gibson's notification to the naval officer was forwarded on the 25th; it was acknowledged as having been received on the 26th at about 6 o'clock.

Anping is bombarded on the 25th. I have never been able to ascertain whether Tseng made due diligence in acquainting the native officers in Taiwanfoo with what had been done and whether the latter, being in the ignorance of the arrangment made, actually made preparations to resist the British. But what is certain is that, on the 25th, from information the naval officer received through a resident of Takao, Mr. Taylor, it appears that the whole village of Anping was filled with armed men; that they had guns in position, and had attempted to reoccupy the village. Therefore the naval officer, acting on this information, sent a Despatch to the Commandant of the Fort: that, unless he retired with his forces before 3 o'clock, he should be obliged to open fire. No answer came up. Therefore, at 4 o'clock, it is said, the naval officer opened fire upon the fortifications. The fire did no damage, the Chinese getting out of the way, as the shells were coming. It has been said that the Commander in chief of the Island, General Lew, had ordered the resistance to which Mr. Taylor's report alluded; and thus that he was responsible for Lt. Gordon's landing. I do not believe it. There is no evidence on record that Chentai Lew gave order to attack and re-occupy Anping. It is true, we know, that he was anxious to do so. But we know also that he was dissuaded by Mr. Man, Commissioner of Customs for Southern Formosa. All he did was to make preparations to oppose the advance of the British further than Anping. He erected stockades, rebuilt such portions of the walls of Taiwanfoo that had been destroyed by the eartquake, and manned them. This he considered he had a perfect right to do under the agreement entered into with Mr. Gibson, Taiwanfoo not having been surrendered to the British forces, and he was in duty bound to reassure the populations greatly alarmed by the presence of Lt. Gordon at Amping.

The display of force of which Mr. Taylor made mention to Lt. Gordon on the 25th can be easily explained. There are in Taiwan no regular forces, except the body guard of the General or field officers commanding at the fortified points over the Island. In Taiwanfoo the

Commandant in Chief has about one thousand braves who are quartered in the interior of the city, in his Yâmen, or near it. The Heptai, or General in command at Anping, has but few of those men, the remainder of his forces consisting of the inhabitants of the place, organ zed as a militia corps and required to wear a sort of soldiers jacket, when on duty. On the 25th, these men were in Anping by the very simple reason that they are there every day in the year, and that they had been especially invited to remain by Mr. Gibson in his proclamations, posted at Amping on the 21st. However, I suspect that their commandant had omitted to order them to put aside their military dress. So that very unfortunatly they appeared in uniform in the streets of the place, which lead Mr. Taylor to suppose that the fort was being reoccupied by the Chinese. The commandant, when leaving his Yâmen, had probably left forty or fifty of his men in charge, being under the impression that there was no harm in doing so. These men Lt. Gordon found when, in the evening, the 25th, having heard that he was to hold Anping on agreement made the day before by Tseug and Mr. Gibson, he determined to land. These men, started up out of their sleep, in the middle of the night, not knowing probably what the whole thing was about, rushed to their arms; and the British officer, acting as any good soldier, in such circumstances would have done, having no means to ascertain what force was in the place, rushed at them so as to leave them no time to organize, and killed a few.

On the 26th, the Heptai who must have heard of what had taken place, and who doubtless was responsible for the occurrence to his superior, hasted to Anping to arrange matters. Lieut. Gordon was, we must not forget, in a very critical position, only twenty three men with no possible support from the ship. He felt that against an avalanche of men that would necessarily crush him if they should come to close quarters, he must take advantage of his arms and operate at long range. So, without giving the enemy time for reflection, they opened fire, killing one man. It is said that the Chinese stood and returned the volley and then fled. The Heptai, who was with them, lost his head, and, in Chinese fashion, poisoned himself.

That was all the fighting. On the 27th, Mr. Gibson arrived at Anping after it was all over. He condemned all the money requisitions made by Lt. Gordon during his absence, holding that any agreement of the sort, in such circumstances, would simply 'e id the Ch nese to believe that foreigners had come to Anping in quest of money and not of justice. As a matter of fact, it belonged to the native me.c iants and the property of the merchants can make no impression upon the feelings of the officials in China. Therefore it would have been a very great hindrance if the British forces had been obliged to advance in Taiwan, an 1 it was not in his request to the naval officer. The senior naval officer, however, on Mr. Gibson's representation, gave back the $40,000 which had been obtained from the native merchants, upon the condition that it would be held by the naval officer as a guarrentee that the Consul's demands should be fulfilled by the local authorities, and he agreed to return the other sums, should the Admiral direct him to do so.

The occurrences on the 25th and 26th gave rise to the question of the responsibility of the Consul for the acts of the naval officer.

The loss of life on the 25th and 26th, destruction of property on the 26th, and money requisitions, which resulted from the action of Lieut Gordon at Anping, all of which was independent of his previous agreement with the Consul, gave rise to a grave question, at the time: the question of the responsibility of the Consul for the acts of the naval officer. It was said justly that when a Consul calls upon a naval commander for support, he assumes thereby the responsibility of the consequences of the armed intervention in its full extent, but I should add, so far only as the plan of action agreed upon should have been carried out entirely. If, after both the naval officer and the Consul have settled upon a plan, the naval officer deviates from it, I should think he does so at his own risk. If it is proved that, in doing so, he has acted judiciously, he must have all the credit; but should the reverse appear, he must be blamed.

Mr. Gibson returns to Taiwanfoo where his conditions, as submitted on the 18th, are considered.

Having a c mplished all this, Mr. Gibson returned to Taiwanfoo where the conditions submitted to Tseng, on the 18th previous, were soon considered and, one after the other, complied with. Thus Tseng, who we remember, had informed the Consul that he had no power to consider these conditions, by his own fault, "was left no alternative but either to admit to the Consul such misrepresentation and derilection of duty in the first instance in not punishing offenses and serious outrages, or a gross pervertion of justice when a settlement was effected in the end, and sentences passed, under such pressure as Mr. Gibson put upon him." (1)

Views of the Anping affair, as taken by the Britsh & American Ministers, and by Lord Clarendon. The Anping affair has been differently judged. In his correspondence with the Tseng lee Yâmen and will Lord Clarendon, H. B. M.'s Minister in China, contended that the whole responsibility of the conflict that took place, on the 25th and 26th, with consequent loss of life and destruction of public property, rested with Liang for the serious provocations so long and so persistently given, and with the Vice Roy and Governor at Foochow, who not only tolerated such continued misgovernment and violation of Treaty, but encouraged them and finally neglected to give effect to the Central Government's orders at the eleventh hour while it was yet time to prevent an appeal to arms and a catastrophe.

Mr. J. Ross Browne, U. S. Minister at Peking, maintained that the instructions of the foreign Governments to their consuls, issued after the signing of the Treaty of Tientsin, had been ignored by Mr. Gibson and he warned me against following on his steps (1).

As to Lord Clarendon he found no words of blame strong enough to condemn Mr. Gibson's conduct at Anping; he wrote to the Minister for England:—"It is quite clear that Mr. Gibson is wholly unfit to be intrusted with any discretionary power or to be placed in any other than a subordinate situation where he will be constantly under the superintendence and control of a superior Consular officer on the spot. His proper office is that of Interpreter, and you will be careful not to place under his charge the superintendence, even temporary, of a consulate or vice consulate, for the duties of which judgment tact, discretion, and moderation are essential requisites.

I need scarcely say that, under no circumstances, must he be allowed to remain in Formosa; and I only hope that the judgment thus passed on his conduct will produce a salutary impression throughout the consular service in China, and serve as a warning to all persons employed in it, that Her Majesty Government will visit with the severest condemnation acts of violence wantonly under taken and carried out without the express sanction of Her Majesty's Government."

---

(1) Sir R. Alcock to Lord Clarendon (unpublished official correspondence.)
(1) Privately, Mr. J. R. Browne held other views.

(89)

My views of the Anping affair. When the intelligence of this sentence passed upon Mr. Gibson reached me, I did all I could to have it reversed. Seeing that he was sick and almost incapable of doing any work—(he died of sorrow, two months afterwards by my side, in Amoy)—and at his request, I wrote his defence in the best manner I could and sent it to our Minister begging him to submit it to his colleage for England. Mr. Browne did so on his return to Peking, in June 1869, and Sir Rutherford Alcock lost no time in communicating with his Government (11th June 1869). But the judgement was never reversed.

The Anping affair taken in connexion with the instructions of the Department of State. I have never known the views which were taken of the Anping affair at Washington; but I have always considered that, under the instructions of the Department to his Agents at Peking, issued many years ago, Mr. Gibson's action in seizing fort Zelandia was justifiable, and therefore I was of the opinion that a commentary upon the first paragraph of these instructions by the Department and which would enable Consuls, in cases of emergency, to judge by analogy of the circumstances under which a resort to force would be justifiable, was all that was required. It reads as follows:—"I feel very sensibly the embarrassments of giving instructions at this distance, which will be applicable to the prevention or settlement of unforeseen local disputes to arise in China. Nevertheless, there are some principles which may be safely adopted.

1. "One of these is, that Consuls ought, in all practical cases, to refer every question to the Legation, and to await instructions there from, before resorting to the expedient of threats or demonstration by force (1)."

Now what is meant by "all practical cases? An emergency I take it to be, an exceptional condition of affairs involving such immediate danger to life or liberty as to leave no remedy by Diplomacy.

In the case before us, as related above, we find that, in May 1868, the house of the compradore of Elles & Co. had been burned down; in June, the Governor of the Island had set a price on Mr. Pikering's head. In July, Mr. Hardy was stabbed in the streets by one of the Yamen's

---
(1) These instructions have not been published that I am aware of.

soldiers. Subsequently reports similar to those that caused the massacre of Tientsin, last year, were spread among the people by persons in the employ of the highest officers in the Island. A catechist was murdered. On the 21st of September, an armed ambuscade was planted on the road to Pitau to capture and kill a Consul and a naval officer. On the 31st of the same month, Dr. Maxwell's house was burned down. We know that from the 17th of August until Anping was taken (20th of November) the foreign residents had all left Taiwanfoo, a treaty port, in fear of their lives, and all trade was de facto suspended therein. It will doubtless be conceded that all this was certainly an exceptional state of affairs and one which, in a country like China, indicates the greatest danger. *But past experience teaches that, in the East, such signs are not deceptive. Therefore they should not be ignored.* And in this lies my argument to show that the condition of affairs, as we take it to have existed in and around Taiwanfoo, on the 20th of November, involved such immediate danger to the life and the property of foreign residents as to leave no remedy short of forcible resistance by reprisals as were made in taking Anping.

Conclusion. The Anping affair being likely to be one of the most important precedents in the events that Consuls may have to examine and understand for their future guidance, I hardly need to make an apology for having so much enlarged upon a subject that does not concern me personally as an officer of the United States and wherein the interests of our country are only indirectly involved, being more or less bound up in the general welfare. If Consuls understand it thoroughly in its connexion with the general principle involved in it, they will be at no loss when called upon to make an application of it. If the question remains unsolved and obscure, we shall be apt to err and, what would be worse, I believe, in China, remain undecided or timid. I have therefore not hesitated in thus giving to you a full exposé of this important case, in order that the state of foreign intercourse with the Chinese may be exhibited in its proper light.

AMOY, March 31st, 1871.

MEMORANDUM No. 5.

A PLAN FOR THE BETTER TRANSACTION OF
FOREIGN AFFAIRS IN THE INTERIOR OF THE EMPIRE BETWEEN
THE CONSULS AND THE CHINESE.

(93)

Memorandum No. 5.

A PLAN FOR THE BETTER TRANSACTION OF FOREIGN AFFAIRS IN THE INTERIOR OF THE EMPIRE BETWEEN THE CONSULS AND THE CHINESE.

拱垂玒報德崇能惟事位賢惟官建
治下天而

He gave offices only to the worthy, and employments only to the able, * * * then he had only to let his robes fall down and fold his hands, and the Empire was orderly ruled (The Shooking, the book of Shang.)

Before going into the subject of reforms to be introduced both in our Consular service and in the branch of chinese administration which is more especially intended for the transaction of foreign affairs in the interior of the Empire and at the treaty ports, we must consider the great points involved in this question: The treaty of Tientsin and the Government of the Chinese.

The great fea- The great feature of the treaty of Tientsin was the
ture of the treaty provision for a Resident Minister at Peking. "Experi-
of Tientsin. ence, since 1842, had made one point clear, that it was utterly futile to make treaties, so long as the foreign powers were debarred access to the Central Government, the only authority desired to be responsible for their observance. While they allowed themselves to be referred, for the adjustment of their intercourse, to an Imperial Commissioner, in the person of the Provincial Governor of Canton, there could be no security for the maintenance of pacific relations. The servant of a central power, intensely hating the foreigner, how dare he do otherwise than give effect to the wish of his masters? to act otherwise would have been to risk life as well as fortune. When, therefore, they applied to him for the fufilment of the stipulations of our treaty, they were simply mocked at. They addressed representations to Peking, but the only answer they could get was a reference back to the Provincial Governor, who, in turn, referred them, for their satisfaction, to the perusal of his own letters.

Tossed to and fro, like a shuttle between Imperial and Provincial authority, our Ministers were unable to make either responsible for the commission of acts of which they had daily to complain. The treaties became a dead letter and, for years, we endured a state of things which practically involved no relations at all with the Chinese Government, as represented by its Canton Commissioner. At last England and France declared war.

Direct relations, as the result of the expedition in 1860, were established with the Imperial Government, and the right for foreigners to trade in the interior of the provinces was again reaffirmed." (1)

Brief sketch of the Government of China.
The country which was thus being opened to us was not what we generally take it to be. It was much more a vast confederation of eighteen provinces, governed by nine Vice-Roys, than an Empire under the ordinary acception of the term and, up to this day, it has not changed. Those Vice-Roys administer their provinces as they choose; make regulations for all internal questions, for the collection of taxes of all natures, for the keeping of armies, for the payment of the salaries of all the civil and military officers of what ever grade they might be. They concentrate, in one word, in their hands, the prerogatives of the Sovereign power itself, including the right of life and death, in certain cases, and that of grace. They are sorts of Proconsuls with both judicial authority and military command (potestates vel jurisdictionem et imperium) and have with Peking no well defined lien. "With all this the Vice-Roys profess the greatest respect for the sacred person of the Emperor. And why would they not? the sovereign does not inconvenience them in the least; he does not interfere in their administration, and seldom takes decisions in matters connected with it, unless it is upon the proposition of the Great Council (2) which is composed of all the friends of the provincial dignitaries from the Tsung-tu to the Tung-chi.

The Vice-Roys, or Governors General, are appointed for three years; they seldom remain longer. The Emperor can remove them from office,

(1) "General remarks upon our policy," by Horatio N. Lay C. B., late Inspector General of Chinese Customs. London 1864.

(2) Kiun 軍 —Ki 機 Ta 大 Chin 臣 (S. S. Williams), the name of the board Kiun 軍 Ki 機 Chu 處 (Baron de Meritens), the place where they meet.

degrade them or censure them, and it is not rare to hear that he has made use of this sovereign privilege." (1)

The Governor-General belongs always to the first class of officers, by his ex-officio dignity of President of the Board of War, a dignity by virtue of which he is enabled to command the military of two provinces. As Governor-General he exercises authority over the civil officers and the people. But, by his side, he has two officers, the Tartar-General or Tsiang-kiun, and the Governor, or Futai with whom he must consult on all matters of importance relating to each of the Provinces composing his Government. The first of these officers, the Tsiang-kiun, of the Emperor's, family and generally of a rank higher than the Governor-General, in the Fookién province, collects the revenue derived from imports and exports, and in other provinces, he commands the Tartar troops, and takes jurisdiction over their families which, at the time of the conquest, were located, as so many military colonies, in a separate ward, inside the walls of the capital of each province in the Empire. "The other officer, the Futai, as ex-officio Vice-President of the Board of War, has a certain number of troops under his command, altogether independent of the Governor-General. In certain cases, which are sufficiently numerous, he issues a death warrant, just as the Governor-General does; and, like the latter, he can, at all times, send a report direct to the Emperor, on any subject, a privilege that would alone place him almost on a virtual equality with the Governor-General, where there is so much to conceal, and so many stories to make up. A distinction in the nature of their duties that the Chinese always make, when questioned on the subject, is, that the Governor-General is almost exclusively concerned in what passes on the rivers and the sea, while the Governor is more immediatly concerned with what passes on the land." (2) All the naval forces are under the immediate control of the Governor-General, although they are under the chief command of an Admiral whose rank is equal to and powers, in time of war, exceed those of the Governor-General.

---

(1) Confidential Report made to the Inspector General of Customs at Peking in 1868, by Baron de Meritens, Commissioner of Customs, at Foochow.

(2) Desultory notes &c. &c. By Thomas Taylor Meadows, Interpreter to her Majesty's Consulate at Canton. London 1847.

The various secretaries at Peking, including the Department of foreign affairs, correspond with these three officers on a footing of perfect equality. Never do they send them orders or imperative Despatches (Chah), but simple communications (Tze-wên). In fact, although vested with the supreme power, neither the Emperor or the Council of State have any taste for what we usually call centralisation. They consider their task easier by assuming less responsibility or even taking any unless they are compelled to. The Governors-General do the same with their Governors, with their Fantai, (1), or Superintendent of Finances, their Niêtais (2), or Provincial Judges, their Yun-tais (3), or Collectors of the salt gabel, their Leang-chu-tau (4) or Grain Collectors, that is to say make them responsible for the execution of the orders given and the established laws. The Governor, in turn, leaves every thing with the Tautais, or Intendants of Circuit (5); and the Tautais with the Che-fu, or Prefects of Departments, and the Chi-fus with the Tung-chis, Sub Prefects and so on to the end of the scale.

(1) The Fantai receives that part of the land tax which is fixed in money, from the District Magistrates or other authorities. They pay it directly into his establishment, and he has, consequently, from the way these things are done in China, a great influence over them. He has, besi es, the privilege of addressing the Emperor directly three times in the year. On two of these occasions the address is said to be merely "congratulatory form," but on the third, he makes a long report on all the affairs of the Province. The standards of weights and measures are deposited in his Yamun. He pay the salaries of all the officers, and those newly appointed must deliver their credentials to him. Besides these, his peculiar duties, he exercises, under the Governor General and the Governor, a general superintendance over all the affairs of the Province.

(2) He can take cognizance of civil actions; but he is more specially a criminal judge and, as such he may be called the highest judicial authority of the province;·for although the Governor General and the Governor, in granting a death—warrant, also examine the criminal, it is merely for form's sake. The judge is the officer usually deputed to quell rebellions against the officers in distant parts of the Province, on which occasions he has the power delegated to him of issuing death warrants; and having the chief command of the troops that accompany him, he has the privilege of addressing the Emperor in the same manner as the Superintendent of Finances.

(3) The authority of the Salt Commissioner is confined to the salt department, and a superintendence over the sale of native iron.

(4) His duty is to superintend the collection of that part of the land tax which is fixed payable in kind, or to name the price and receive the amount of so much as may ultimately be demanded in money. He also acts as a kind of commissary general, superintending the distribution of their rations to the military throughout the province.

(5) There are many of these in each Province; one is stationed in each of the several circuits into which it is unequally divided. The office of Tautai unites in itself, in a manner similar to that of Governor General and that of Governor, a direct general superintendence over all the affairs of a circuit, not excluding those of a military nature (Desultory notes &c. T. Taylor Meadows, quoted above.)

The Chinese Laws, made to secure the just administration of the Provinces, are many; but, owing to the extent of the conntry, they are powerless in checking the rapacity or dishonesty of the officials. Hence the provinces of this Great Empire, like those of Rome, have been miserably oppressed by the exactions of their officers without possible interference on the part of the Central power, if we can so call it. In this manner not only the avarice of the Governors has to be gratified, but that of all his officers. In all matters of finances the Governors General are like large Farmers on whom the Master, the Emperor, draws for his personal wants and the wants of his court and whenever he thinks fit to do so; but, heavy as his wants are, the Governors General are able to still retain the lion's share.

One of the Imperial privileges is to send Imperial dignitaries, with an honorific rank, among the various Governors General, for them to dispose of, and it is this corps of functionaries without offices, who constantly ask for employment and must be provided for, that constitutes one of the most trying sores of the Empire. Most of these expectant officers are located at the barriers in the interior to collect the local taxes and they remain there till an employment suitable to their grade is found for them (1).

Such as it is this old mechanism had been able to stand till now and to work both good and bad without bringing much difficulty to the Peking Government, or disturbances to its ever cherished quietude. The resources of the provinces have seldom failed in any alarming proportion. The rebellions have been overwhelmed; and it is likely that when we come to force upon Peking any serious occupation beyond the care of the coasts, the Imperial Government will refuse to accept for itself alone and constituted as it is, from the foreign powers, a responsibility which, from their want of knowledge of the distant provinces, they are unprepared to take. A few instances may demonstrate this thoroughly.

(1) Most of this revenue is expended in paying the salaries of the expectant officers and in defraying extraordinary expenses, such as the suppression of revolts, the erection of public works &c. The Arsenal of Foochow has been partially built from local taxes levied in the Province of Fuhkien. Of the duties collected from the salt, the junk trade, the foreign maritime customs, about seven tenths are lodged in the Governor General's treasury and are spent in defraying public provincial expenses. The balance is sent to Peking where it is distributed between the Emperor, his family and the manchu nobles living yet in manchuria, (conversations with admiral Lee, a native officer.)

"The Governor General of the Kiangs who generally resides at Nankin, is the Imperial Commissioner for foreign affairs, although the Ministers Plenipotentiary of the Great Powers reside at Peking. To the present day, the Emperor has refused to accept a single suggestion made by Europe or America even in the interest of China, unless it was backed up by one of these great dignitaries. The famous Osborne flotilla, the original plan of which had been given by Mr. Hart, or the present French Arsenal at Foochow, were approved only after they had been presented and endorsed by their Vice Roys. The first scheme was proposed by Tseng-kwo-fan, the then Governor General of Nankin, and the second by Tso Kong-pao, the then Governor General of Fohkien and Chi-kiang, who, although now out of his Vice Royalty, is still responsible for the success of the enterprise. On the other side the only great scheme which had been originated exclusively under Imperial patronage and outside of the Governor General, the Peking college, has failed" (1).

But above the Emperor or the Governors General are the literary men who, like the Brames once in India, the Roman Priests in Europe, in an occult manner, through craft and deceit, ruled the people. To them we have nothing to oppose but a will of iron, a skill superior to their own and the moral influence of our Missionaries who may yet pave a road to civilisation in China, as their precursors, the first apostles, have done during the first ages of Christianity, within the limits of the Roman Empire, before it fell to pieces, an easy prey to the barbarians of the North (2).

The treaty stipulations. Such was the Government whose task it was to give effect to the treaties of Tientsin modified as they were by the convention held at Shanghai six months, I believe, after they had been signed. The most important stipulations of these treaties were, first, the right for foreign merchants to travel to all parts of the Empire under a system of passports for the purpose of trade or of pleasure. Secondly the right to send or take foreign goods into, or bring foreign owned produce, from, the interior, under a system of transit passes.

---

(1) Baron de Meritens' confidential report, &c. &c. quoted above.

(2) I have not made any mention here of the six Supreme Boards and of the board of Civil Office in Peking, those details being purely administrative and they can be found in most all the books on China.

Right of travel in the interior for the purpose of pleasure or trade. In the first clause we grasped with one of the most serious and one of the most just objections made by China to our Diplomatists: The difficulty for her officers to enforce the laws and the police regulations of the country with foreigners who are not subject to her jurisdiction, who do not speak her language, and who, most often, escape punishment after they have been turned over to their Consuls.

It is true that we may reply to China that, in this, she suffers the consequences arising from the state of semi—barbarism in which she is, there being no justice in the Empire and the tortures applied to those undergoing examinations before her courts, shock our morals and conflict with our civilisation. But whatever may be the value of this argument and the right we may have to put it forward, we should prefer, conciliating the healthy principles laid down in the treaties, with the respect due to the laws and the customs of the nation into whose territories we have come to reside, acknowledge the correctness of the objection made, and, in an additional rule, find, if possible, the remedy to the situation made to us.

Foreign Interpreters appointed, with judicial powers, to Governors-General &c. Executive part of the service. To meet the requirements of the case, I would apply to the inland districts a system of justice somewhat similar to that which has been so successfully introduced at the Treaty Ports to regulate the relations which, of necessity, had to exist there since the signing of the treaties, between the native revenue authorities and the merchants. I would appoint to the Vice-Roys, Governors and Tautais at each port open to foreign trade, interpreters of foreign birth, whose chief business would be to assist the local authorities in the transaction of foreign affairs at the treaty Ports and in the interior districts visited by tourists, missionaries and merchants. They would be vested with judical powers to act jointly with the native officers, in all cases arising within the limits of their respective districts.

Rules of procedure &c. The rules of procedure to be observed in such cases would be laid down by means of special legislation and they would form a code of laws to be approved by all the representatives of the foreign powers and promulgated, like any other Laws, by the central native Government at Peking, through its Governors-General; and it would be so construed that it could apply to all cases, both Civil or

Criminal, with right of appeal, in first instance, to a higher authority at the nearest treaty Port, and, as a last resort, to a Supreme Court to be held at various points of the Empire as I will soon explain. "As a preventive measure it would be well, I believe, to enact that the penalty provided in Article 48 of the British treaty of Tientsin, against vessels engaged in smuggling, will apply to any one who, having received leave to travel in the interior of the Empire, either for purposes of pleasure or of trade, should have seriously abused the privileges given to him, or otherwise violated the laws and regulations of China. Such person, being arrested by the native authorities, as the treaty provides, would be turned over to the competent local authorities, to be tried and, if convicted, could have his passport cancelled never to receive an other, and, in case of a very serious offence, upon requisition made by the Central Government, he would be expelled for ever from the Empire. Such a penalty made to strike the guilty parties in their future prospects and in their fortunes would constitute one of the greatest guarantees against bad behavior from those who really have any thing to lose. At first those against whom the authorities might have to take steps would be of that class of adventures for whom it is difficult to profess any sympathy. The object of a treaty of commerce is not to protect such people, but to give assistance and facility to those really engaged in trade, and who have interest in being in good terms with all and to quarrel with none. I believe that, had we offered such guarantee to China in 1858, we should have had very little trouble in bringing her to give us free access to the interior, there to reside and to trade; for she would have soon learned by experience that she could always look for the prompt trial and punishment of those of our people who would have abused of a right frankly asked and liberally conceded."(1)

Merits of the plan proposed. In this manner the right of original jurisdiction of which, with reason, the Chinese are so jealous, would be returned to them; and the principle, laid down by Mr. Cushing, and whereby a foreign state, under any circumstances must be denied jurisdiction over the lives and liberties of citizens of the United States, unless that foreign state be of our own family, in a word, a Christian State, would also be fully respected. Again the authority of these officers being sufficient to insure the maintainance of order, the reasons offered as an excuse by

---

(1) Baron de Meritens' confidential report &c. &c., quoted above.

the Chinese for excluding us from the interior, that we are not amenable to any laws and often take advantage of it to disregard the feelings or the rights of the people, or show disrespect to the local authorities, and that it is almost impossible to produce proof against us in the consular courts at the treaty ports, and that the immunity, which we thus enjoy, is productive of regrettable conflicts between the Vice-Roys and the Consuls, would thus be removed. The salutary influence of the Interpreters would not be less felt in an other direction. The native officers, feeling that their acts are controlled and watched by men that cannot either be deceived or bribed, could no longer refuse to meet the foreign applicants for redress, on fair grounds and they must act as their conscience, threnceforth enlightened by sound and responsible advices, may dictate.

As to the relations existing between the native authorities and the Interpreters, they would be those which now govern the official interconse of the Commissioners of Customs with the Haiquans. There should be no subordination of the Chinese officer to the Interpreter. There would not be even an assimilation of rank between them. One, the native officer, might, as the Haiquan now is, be considered as having the command under the Tsenglee Yamén whose orders, the other, the Interpreter, must see executed. In this manner any opinion, as expressed by the latter, would be expected to receive the respectful consideration of the former, and, although it is admitted that room for differences between them must often be left, in such cases and in unforeseen emergencies, they could not fail to agree upon the course to be adopted, and to cooperate with each other to the best of their abilities. Both would be responsible to their respective superiors for their opinions and their acts, and they would correspond directly and separately with them on the subject of public foreign affairs.

Instructions concerning Chinese political questions, as distinguished from those purely foreign would be intrusted, at they now are, to the care of native officials, without possible interference on the part of the Interpreters, and the Emperor's commands would be conveyed to both through the regular channel. However, responsibilities of a peculiar character would devolve upon the Interpreters, as they would be made aware of from time to time, by their immediate superiors at Peking.

As to the rank of the officer called to direct the working of the foreign branch of this new service at Peking, no suggestions could be made; the susceptibilities and the vanity of the Chinese not being likely to remain indifferent in the settlement of this question, it should be discretely left for the contracting parties to decide. The creation of this new service might be also the pretext for the introduction of a desirable reform in the customs service of the Empire. The circumstances which rendered the establishment, in 1855, of the foreign branch of this administration, having in a great measure, passed away, there is hardly any reason why it should not be fused into the native branch under one chief, a Chinese, with the present Commissioners, assisted by two Secretaries, one foreign and the other native, as Interpreter-advisors. This, however, could not be accomplished, but gradually and as the vacancies which might conveniently be made by the appointment of foreign officers, now in the Customs employ, to the positions of Interpreters to territorial officers, could be filled by natives whose fitness for the position would be ascertained by severe examination in one of the foreign languages spoken in the East and the other branches of requisite knowledge. In this manner the present system of compensation by means of fixed salaries, adopted in the present foreign branch of the service, could be gradually applied to the whole native administration and the demoralizing system of squeezes would, in the long run, come to an end.

The controlling part of the service. So much for the executive part of this service. As to the controlling branch, which is the most important of all, it would consist of eight officers of high rank residing at Peking, four Foreign and four Chinese, all well versed in Chinese and English or French. Six months in the year these officers would make tours of inspection in both the Northern and Southern divisions of the Empire. They would be expected, with others of an equal rank, foreigners, who would be called Inspectors of Consulates, appointed by each Power, to inspect the Consular Districts, and to adjust all cases which, owing to legal or other difficulties, from time to time, must be left open for final adjudication by a higher court. These officers, somewhat resembling, for the occasion, those whom the Roman Emperors sent to command in distant Provinces, in cases of great emergency (Legati Cesaris) would have exceptional powers, and when absolutely required, the foreign associate concurring, would have power to suspend officers of any rank. On their return to Pekin they would make their report which, if advisable, might be published for the information of the Ministers, of the Consuls and of the public.

This plan is entirely Chinese. The advantage of this plan is that it is essentially Chinese. We remember that the Chinese Magistrates do not officiate in the Provinces of their birth, and all the official business is transacted in the mandarin language which is spoken only in some of the northern provinces. Consequently there is no official in the Empire that has not his judicial Interpreter and advisor or Shi-ye 師爺. "The sole business of these people is to protect the interests of their employer, to point out to him the proper way of conducting his judicial examinations; and to see that the decisions he pronounces are in strict accordance with the laws and justified by the facts of each particular case, so that he may not incur any of the penalties laid down in the code of the board of civil office. To obviate this, too, all documents that issue from a Yamun, are revised by these men, and those of importance are drafted by them." (1) The only difference between the She-ye and the Foreign Judicial Interpreters, as I propose them to be would be that, while the former are not recognized by the Government as official servants, the latter would be and they would hold their appointment from the Emperor. Unlike their native colleagues they would have an official seat at judicial examinations in cases involving foreign interests, and, although no judgment would be rendered in their name, no decision in any cases would be final and could be appealed from to a higher Court, unless it is concurred in by them, and they would be held responsible both by the provincial authorities and their superiors at Peking for the opinions given and the judgments rendered by the native officers at their suggestion.

The substitution of regular salaries for the present system of "squeezes" is also eminently conformable to Chinese usage and laws, which, in this special reference, stand in direct contradiction to the actual practice, which is so universal now that we have taken it for the law. The most revered principles of legislation reprove, in the strongest manner, the low standard at which the salaries of the public officers are fixed as the ultimate cause of the evil we have signalized. As we have seen, it is written: "When officers display capacity and activity, promote their

(1) Desultory notes &c. by T. T. Meadows page 105.

views, and the country will be prosperous. All the magistrates being well paid, insist on their doing good; if you cannot render them comfortable in their own families, these men will soon be involved in crimes (take improper means to supply their wants)." (Shooking, Book IV, section V. written B. C. 1121). And again: "If you regularly in giving your orders say, "My instructors whom I am to follow, my minister of instruction, my minister of war, and my officers of works; my heads of departments, and all ye, my officers, I will on no account with oppressions put men to death." Let the prince also set the example of respecting and encouraging the people, and these will proceed to respect, and encourage them. Let him go on in dealing with those who have been traitors and villains, murderers and harbourers of criminals, to exercise pardon, and these, when they observe the prince's conduct, will likewise pardon those who have assaulted others and injured their property. When sovereigns appointed Inspectors, they did so in order to the government of the people * * * * (Shooking,—fifth part, Book XI. The Timber of the Tsze tree Translated by James Legge, D. D., Hongkong, 1865).

Interior trade. I now come to the second stipulation, viz: the privilege for foreign merchants to carry goods in transitu from or to the interior, on payment of one half of the tariff duty, the advantage of this being that it exempts them from the local taxes paid by Chinese at each barrier, on exports, from the place of production to the place of exportation and, on imports, from the port of entry to the place of consumption.

"This article of the treaty, on the main land, in this province, has seldom received even a show of execution." (1)

Chinese objections to interior trade being conducted according to treaty stipulations.

It is true that the Foreign Board at Peking has, several times, ordered ostensibly in the most imperative manner that the transit passes should be respected everywhere in the interior of the country; but their commands, soon followed by secret instructions, have not received generally any consideration. And this is easy to conceive: "For when the Governors-General saw that they would have to communicate to the Peking authorities, the account of taxes that are collected in the interior on imports or exports, and which, under the farming system, they themselves ignore and have no interest to know; when it became evident to

(1) Baron de Meritens' confidential report &c. &c., quoted above.

(105)

them that the result of the substitution of the new system for the old one, would be the ruin of the army of expectant officers for whose maintainance they are answerable to the Emperor, and the signal of reclamations which they would be unable to satisfy; when it became not less evident for the Governors-General that the presence of foreigners in the interior would give rise to endless difficulties which they had no means to settle, and which would be the means of bringing to light fiscal transactions in which they have never been and could not possibly be interfered with, a pain of being made responsible for extortions which, for centuries, they had both permitted and shared; when finally the Tseng-lee Yamén understood that, by all this, they would deeply hurt the feelings of the Emperor's representatives in certain Provinces and give a strong shock to the whole administrative machine for which they have so much respect and fancy, and which, in fact, they cannot change but by order of the Emperor acting with the consent and by the advice of the Great Council, they all entered into a tacit agreement to bury the subject of transit dues and to leave it as an open question never to be solved if possible." (1)

In this Province they closed the discussion by entirely setting aside the treaty stipulations, it being held by some that the tenth article of the British Treaty of Nanking refers only to merchants and not to merchandize, and by others, that it is of no avail to either. As to the IX article of the British Treaty of Tientsin confirmed by rules 7th and 8th of the American supplementary Treaty of Shanghai, of 1858, they held that it refers only to travel for the purpose of pleasure and they have refused permission to travel for purposes of trade. Or when they gave that permission, in Formosa, for instance, they submitted the operators to so many tribulations that they had to withdraw from the trade. For instance, in 1868, having yielded to me as regards passports, they took advantage of an obcure point in the treaty by placing on all foreign owned goods, in transitu, a tax which was not levied on goods in native hands; and the spirit of the Treaty of Tientsin, the framers of which contemplated that chinese and foreign merchants should be placed on equal terms, was disregarded thereby. Later, they admitted by proclamation that foreign merchants had a right to evade the local taxes by sending their goods into the interior under the authorized transit certificates; but at the same time, they directed their

---

(1) Baron de Meritens confidential report &c. &c. quoted above.

officers to stop goods in transitu under the most futile pretexts, to make the native servants of the owners of the goods responsible for any alleged breach of the regulations, and they announced that no claim would be intertained for deterioration of goods or loss of weight or market, and they privately informed the Chinese consignees that, in the event of their receiving such goods, their hongs should be shut and their goods confiscated.

Revision of the Treaty as proposed by Sir R. Alcock & Mr. Hart. Sir R. Alcock, H. B. M.'s Minister at Peking, and Mr. Robert Hart, Inspector General of the Foreign Customs, have proposed to meet the difficulty arising from this state of affairs, by increasing considerably the duties on opium, and those on imports and exports by one half, and collecting the same through the foreign branch of the Maritime Customs where certificates, intended to be protective against further taxation in the interior, would be delivered on payment of these additional duties, and where an effective system for refunding charges, illegally levied, would be organized. These able gentlemen think that, thus, the Chinese would be enabled to define the inland taxes and to protect the foreign Merchants against the other abuses connected with the inland trade. They argue that the increase of duty on opium and other merchandize would cause no loss whatever to our merchants, who have interest in obtaining a uniform tariff and who would certainly not pay more under a raised tariff than they now do, as the difference between duties, as now collected, and those that it is proposed to establish and to collect directly from the foreign importer, is now indirectly received from the Chinese dealers under the name of local taxes.

Objections to the British Minister's plan. There is a great deal to say against this plan; but the main objection to it is that it conflicts with the interests of the small mandarins in the interior who, as we have seen, live from the collection of these taxes. If, as proposed, they were shut out from this source of revenue and left with a salary which, when it is paid, is hardly sufficient to defray the yearly expenses of one of their hundred attendants and employés, in self defence, they must continue to collect the old taxes at each barrier, and, in spite of the orders from Peking, they have to ignore the transit passes or other foreign documents exactly as they did after the framing of the treaty of 1858.

It must be remembered that, under the present system, bad as it may be said to be, our merchants have the option to either pay, in addition to the regular import or export duties, to the foreign Commissioner of Chinese Customs, the half tariff duties on all the goods which they desire sending to, or taking from, the interior markets, that they may be freed from further taxation at the inland barriers, or, not to pay these half tariff duties, and, in that case, submit to the native taxation as if they were chinese operators. But, as they have found that the payment made to the foreign branch of the Chinese Customs is not taken into consideration and they are invariably required to settle the taxes at the inland barriers, they never apply for transit certificates or customs memos and they use native agents who simply pay the taxes at the inland barriers. But this they could not do, we must remember, if the plan proposed by H. B. M.'s Minister and Mr. Hart, were adopted; for, in that case, there is no option left to them and they must pay both the duties and the taxes to the foreign Commissioner of Customs, *against a promise* that their goods shall be permitted to circulate free of further taxation throughout the whole Empire. How then, setting aside the opposition of a certain class of Mandarins which, we have seen above, is irrepressible; how, I may be permitted to demand, can the Chinese keep their promise, if the interior taxation is maintained? How will the distinction between goods in foreign and native hands, be made? Is not the experience of the days that followed the signing of the British treaty of 1842 present to our memory? I am well aware that a certain protection must be derived from the refunding system. Yet, how will the merchants prove that they have been wronged in cases of squeezes for which, we well know, receipts are never given?

Such is the plan offered to the trade, for its acceptance, by the noble Minister and his able coadjutor. It can be summed up in a few words: Under the existing treaties, we are paying but *one;* under the new rule, we must expect to have to pay *three!* Further comment is needless; and sooner than see the United States assent to such a legislation, I would rather see our merchants fated to forever live under, the *protective* stipulations of the Treaties of 1858.

Other suggestions discussed. The suggestion made that a solution of the problem before us be found in the abolition of the local taxes as being contrary to the existing Treaties, cannot be better entertained.

China, under the Laws of Nations, has a perfect right to regulate her internal revenue as the pleases, and, as well as any other countries, she must have internal taxes to defray her internal expenses. But, if she cannot be required to abolish those taxes, certainly it can be demanded of her to harmonize them with treaty stipulations that they may cease to be prohibitive, and to equalize them, that the balance of trade will not be disturbed. To this end Baron de Meritens, the able Commissioner of Customs at Foochow, has recommended to fix the taxes throughout the whole Empire at one half of the tariff duties, as inscribed in the convention of Shanghai, of 1858; and, to reconcile conflicting interests, while he advocates the creation of a refunding system under the foreign branch of the Maritime Customs, he wisely leaves the collection of the taxes to the Proviucial Authorities.

In this manner all the requirements of the case, except such as refers to the exaction of squeezes, are met; but this deficiency would be supplied by the Interpreter-Judges and the Inspectors by, and the mixed code in accordance with which all commercial, civil and even criminal cases which may arise between foreigners and Chinese, as I have proposed, should be judged. In sum, I should incline to strongly roommend this combination as being the most simple, the most complete and one that reconciles itself more thoroughly with the Customs and adapts better to the interior economy of the Chinese Empire.

The right of navigation of the great rivers and on the coast. I now come to the subject of navigation of the great rivers in the interior, and of the coast. I have, I confess, very little experience of the former as neither in Formosa nor in the Amoy District proper have we any rivers of any magnitude. But I may say that I am of the opinion that it would be much to the interest of trade to have inserted in our treaty that the natives have the privilege to purchase or build and to own and use for themselves or others, vessels propelled by steam. The Chinese who are very speculative by nature, would soon overcome their prejudices and acquire steam tugs to tow native craft carrying produce on the rivers or on the coast for shipment at the treaty ports. In this manner the coasts and the rivers would become a roadstead opened indirectly to foreign trade and the ports on the coasts or on the rivers navigable to coasting craft would be the last barrier, under rule 7 of the Treaty, through which the merchants could convey to the nearest treaty ports, goods purchased in the interior, or the first barrier through which they would have to pass in case of imports. But should the prohibition to natives to own and use (1) in the transportation of foreign owned goods in transit, boats of foreign model and propelled by steam or by wind, or by foreign hands, be maintained, the suggestion made the year before last that foreign owned cargo boats equipped by natives and duly registered both at the Consulate and at the native Customs, could be used for coast services, would be most acceptable. The native boats are unsafe and their arrangements exceedingly awkward. Many important points of the coast, in my district, for instance the camphor ports of Formosa, Owlan, Goché, are not accessible but in light draft boats, and should the concession asked for be refused, the foreign trade would remain excluded of the best marts on the coast of Formosa which would remain exclusively accessible to native merchants A concession in that direction would have the great advantage of dispensing with the considerable and unnecessary expenses inherent to the opening of new ports, such as Chin-chiew, to the northward of Amoy, and Goché, Owlan and Sau-o-Bay in Formosa. It is also evident that the more foreign commerce will use the coast as a roadstead, the less considerable, at first, the inland travel will be, and this is not of small importance to the Chinese Governors-General to whom the presence of the foreign merchants in the interior, before a proper system of control has been placed in running order, must be the cause of considerable embarrasement and anxiety.

The change recommended would not affect materially the internal economy of the Empire since all the heavy labor would have to be done by natives. Against local exactions, the foreign traders could find sufficient means of redress in the local tribunals constituted upon a new footing, as above stated; and to save the coolies against all possible injustice, a rate of wages not unreasonably exceeding the tariff of the locality as applying to labor performed in the usual indolent way for Chinese merchants, might be agreed upon between the natives and consular authorities. The right of appeal against such decisions, to higher courts, has been fully reserved in the suggestions which I have offered in connection with inland trade; and the privilege for foreigners to appear before the

---

(1) Such prohibition will obtain untill the Great Council of the Empire has proclaimed that such inventions are contained in the kings. See the Canon of Shun, Shoo-king, Book 1st, Section 2, also the Doctrine of the Mean chap. XXVIII.

native magistrates through their native agents in conformity with the custom which obtains with Literati of certain rank, or, if in person, without submitting to ceremonial not prescribed by consular courts, would be also reserved.

The limits of the Treaty Ports. I have not said anything in these notes concerning the right to reside and trade in the open ports. It involves one point of importance which has never yet been determined: the limits of the Treaty Ports. As this would be of secondary importance if the reforms which I have recommended above were adopted, I will not touch upon it.

Currency. I have explained in my various reports to both the Secretaries of State and of the Treasury the want of a uniform currency in China. The disputes which daily arise out of the use of Sycee (1) might be a sufficient cause for pointing out to the cabinets of Peking the advantages of our monetary system.

Tonnage dues. It remain, for me to speak of the Tonnage—Dues funds. One of the most regrettable results of Mr. Hart's irresponsible autocracy has been the waste which, in some instances, has been attendant of the use of these funds. By the terms of the Treaty, they should have been spent in lighting and buoying the China coasts, under the joint supervision of the Chinese Superintendents of Trade and of the Consuls. I find no fault with our able Ministers in so modifying the treaties that the Consuls have ceased to be consulted on these matters; but as, surely, the Inspector General is not more competent than the Consuls to deal with a subject which is of an Engineer's province, I should suggest the propriety of making new arrangements by which these revenues should be placed at the disposal of a mixed commission consisting of Chinese and Foreigners qualified for the work, and who would from time to time draw up statements for the information of the Chinese and foreign Governments. I calculate that the total amount of the Tonnage-Dues received by Mr. Hart, from 1865 to 1868, was about *Taels* 20,000, or about $30,000, per annum, as but one tenth of the sum, collected during that period from foreign trade on account of Tounage-Dues, was handed to the Inspector-General by the Chinese.

---

(1) A Sycee is an ingot of pure silver, having the shape of a shoe. All duties are paid in shoes of Sycee or their equivalents in Mexican Dollars. The Chinese claim that the Mexican Dollars are made of bad silver and when duties are paid in that kind of money they invariably require a bonus of ten per cent.

From the 1st of April 1868, the proportion of the Tonnage-Dues fund for appropriation to the lighting and buoying of the coast of China, was increased to seven tenths, and therefore the amount paid to the Inspector General from that date until the corresponding date of 1871, must have been about *Taels*, 150,000, or, for the three years, *Taels*, 450,000, equal to about $700,000.

Again, the Inspector General received from the British-Government, in liquidation on account of the Osborn flotilla, the sum of £120,000, or $600,000: *Total to the debit of the Tonnage-Dues account, about* $1,390,000.

To the Credit of this account, we must place $210,000, the estimated cost of three beacons at Foochow, the amount already expended for a lighthouse in course of erection at Amoy, a few buoys and beacons at Amoy, Tamsuy and Kelung, Light-ships and beacons at New-chwang, a Light-house and Light-ships at Shanghai (the estimated values of which are *Taels* 36.000). And this amount of $210,000 will swell to $610,000 if we include the coast of three Revenue-Cruisers, purchased in England for £80,000, *leaving a balance of* $780,000 *to the debit of the Tonnage-Dues account.*

If, as Admiral Rowan understood from the Chinese authorities, in 1868, the Government is too poor to go on more energetically with the work of lighting the coast, it must be that this balance of $780,000 has been spent, as I have said in my Report on the trade of my District for the period from September 30th 1868 to September 30th 1869, in supporting an army of idle functionaries who are enumerated in *Memo No.* 5 *(without date) for Marine Commissioners guidance,* issued from the Inspector-General's office; for we cannot take into account the wages of the officers and crews of the three Revenue Ccuizers, two of which have been laid up at Canton ever since they arrived from England, and the third has been lying at anchor in the Amoy harbour, opposite the U. S. Consulate, for the last nine months, regardless of the amount of smuggling which was going on in native junks in the vicinity of the Port and which might have been checked in a measure, had the necessary orders been issued by the Inspector General.

Consular reforms. Having come to this point, it remains for me to speak of the changes which the adoption of the reforms in the branch of the Territorial Administration of the Chinese for the transaction of foreign affairs would require in our own Consular service. And indeed these changes would not be advisible were not corresponding modifications in the Consular service introduced.

In one of my Despatches to the Minister, I have sug-
The grouping of Consulates. Limited centralisation. gested the grouping of the Consulates so that men of weight and experience would be located at the most important points where, or near which, the Governors General reside, and where they would control the minor ports in their respective Districts; they would be in a position to approach the highest Provincial native officers and discuss with them the great questions of internal improvement and trade, which, we have seen, must be solved through them with the central Government at Peking. I say, *must*, because in a country as large as China, the centralisation cannot be absolute and the power although concentrated in the capital, ought to extend, through the Vice Roys, to the extremities of the Empire, that it may be felt there. In this respect the Vice Roys resemble somewhat the Governors of English Colonies or those of our States in America; and in my opinion this system of limited centralisation is so good, so well adapted to the country, that it should not be changed.

Inconvenience of the System of absolute non-local interference. As we have it now with the principle of non-local interference, in any case, and of invariable reference to Peking, nothing is done. In one side we have the Chinese officers who generally are thoroughly ignorant of the treaty stipulations and of the details of the foreign cases coming under their investigation. Secluded in their Yamen, they hear very little or nothing of the outside world, leaving to their confidential secretaries the responsibility of carrying on the duties of their office. The latter knowing well the partiality of their masters for quiet life, generally keep them in the dark till the mob gathers growling in anger at the Yamen door or the cannon of foreigners roars in the distance, threatening a stronger argument than that commonly used with reasonable and thinking people. On the other side the expenses incurred in putting down rebellions have been so heavy and the insurgents have so often been near success that with the phantoms of popular troubles, the Vice-Roys of Provinces carry almost all their points at the Tseng-Lee Yamen which is seldom moved from lethargy and profound indolence except by fear of war with foreign powers.

(113)

Advantages of a System of limited local interference. Native and foreign Inspectors in Chinese employ.
Now that China claims a seat among the western nations, she cannot help frankly accepting the position made for her by the fortunes of war, and decidedly, her rulers cannot expect us to demand from them less than a just and disinterested mediator would claim from us, under the treaties, and the laws of nations. My own experience in Formosa leads me to believe that under the system of limited local action recommended by me a great many misunderstandings must be avoided and a greater harmony of views must prevail. In their special capacity the Inspectors acting as the deputies of the Tseng-lee Yamèn, would be capable of carrying through what the foreign custom house officers, or a Consul of one power, in an almost unofficial capacity, and as friends to both parties, with Consuls of another power often in vain have attempted doing.

Objections to Custom's officers' interference between the Consuls and the native authorities.
It is always a matter of the utmost delicacy for a Consul to so interpose between the Chinese and one of his colleagues even when he is asked to do so by either or both; and but very few will ever accept the responsibility. As for custom house officers to go out of their proper sphere, which is simply to collect the revenue, and, with the best intentions, to peep into the conference room or any other scene of action, and watch the acts of either party, it is a most dangerous task. If by it the Commissioner promotes the end of Justice and serves the foreign cause to the satisfaction of the Chinese, he will gain credit at the Tseng-Lee-Yâmen and may be rewarded. But if matters turn against the Consul, the storm raised against the ill fated mediator must be such as very few can stand. He will be accused in every way by a prejudiced public, which, too often, judging only from appearances, will look at him as if his chief motives had been simply to bring about mischief that he may distinguish himself, afterwards, as a demon of disorder.

As a general thing the Commissioner's interference is seldom desired by the Chinese, and the Consul never accepts it but as a last resort; and this not only because of his natural inclination to maintain his own dignity, or of any prejudices against the foreign branch of the Imperial Customs, but, and chiefly on account of, the gap which the Commissioner's well calculated reticence on all questions where public interest is at stake, the absence of any definite responsibility to either the Chinese or the Foreign Authorities, and the want of a clearly defined sphere of duties for himself and the service over which he presides, have created everywhere, except perhaps at Shanghai, Foochow and Canton, between himself and the Consular body.

The system of absolute non interference judged by its results. The result of this is clear, the wisest and ablest Commissioners, acting in self defence, in critical cases, refuse to act at all; and the native officer left to himself with a subject which he has but imperfectly studied, to discuss with the Consul (a man whose motives he seldom appreciates), being unable to argue, indiscriminately opposes and refuses, till both parties, weary of resistance, come to some sort of compromise, generally unsatisfactory to all concerned, or refer the point in dispute to Peking, with such conflicting statements and obscure records, that it is almost a superhuman task to draw anything like truth from them. Hence endless correspondences and references from the Capital to the Provinces and from the latter to the former which only lead to disappointment and regrets. The judges finally, having to decide in the dark, almost invariably come to conclusions seldom reflecting the credit which their labours and perseverance deserve. As to the merchants, tired of claiming redress in vain, they have ceased to address the Consuls or Ministers whose ability to protect them a bitter experience has taught them to distrust, and, while this is going on, the vigilant Chinese, watching his chance and encouraged by impunity, every day inflicts upon us new wrong.

The Inspectors of Consulates: their functions. The creation of the office of Inspector of Consulates would be the signal of radical improvement in this state of affairs. It would be the means of connecting more closely the provinces to the capital; and the reports which would be made by the Inspectors to the Ministers would have the most salutary effect upon the latter. Isolated as the foreign Ministers are in Peking and inhaling an atmosphere of prejudice and routine, they require, I believe, to be placed under a counterbalancing influence of some sort. It has been said that able as a general may be, he will never accomplish anything if, under him, he has not one that can proceed where he ought to be and yet where he is prevented from going, that can see that which is out of his sight and which still it is important he should know, and that can handle whatever is shaking and which, at the same time, is beyond the reach of the chief

(115)

strong hand. This applies with equal propriety to a Minister in China. His supervision, extending over an immense space, offers no less difficulties than are met by an officer directing the complicated and extensive manœuvres of armies in the field; and while, of necessity, the former is in Peking, watching his chances to carry out the policy of the Government, he cannot direct the minor branches of the service in the Provinces, unless under him, he has one that can see that his plans are well understood, his instructions properly obeyed and the laws strictly executed. This duty the Inspector would perform. He would visit the Ports or such of them as, in his estimation, required his presence, six months in the year, and he would arrange that his tours of inspection corresponded with those of the officers in the employ of the Chinese engaged in a similar labor. In cases of appeal from a Consular Court, in connection with the Chinese officers, he would decide as Supreme Judge.

Advantages offered by the substitution of the Inspectors of Consulates, acting as supreme judges in cases of appeals from a Consular Court, for a Superior Court either at Shanghai or at San Francisco.

This system of appeal presents, I believe, great advantages over that recommended by our able Consul-General, Mr. George F. Seward. Mr. Seward originally proposed to remedy the present evils by the establishment of a Superior Court at Shanghai for China, Japan and Siam, and last year, by reasons of economy, I suppose, he has so far modified his original plan in the bill that passed the Congress of the United States, that all the appeals from the Consular and Ministerial Courts, in the countries above named, must be sent to the California court. I must say that, in my humble opinion, either plan meets but very unperfectly the requirements of the case. I should prefer to either of those plans the substitution of the Inspector of Consulates, who, in addition to his other duties, as defined above, could very well, on the spot and better than either the Consul General as Judge of appeal or the Supreme Court of California, take cognizance of all the cases that would not have been finally decided in Consular Courts. To him all Consuls would be subordinate with right of appeal to the Minister, in political or purely Consular cases.

Indeed, while the facilities afforded to appeal to the Supreme Court of California, will secure, I confess, a desirable redress against errors in the Consular Courts, it is to be feared that the delays and expenses incurred in carrying cases before it, the impracticability, acknowledged in the bill passed, to bring testimony before it from Siam, Japan, Canton and Tientsin, &c., must prevent the majority of our citizens from going before it. On the whole, I think that there is little or nothing, save what I have proposed above, to be changed in the working of our Consular Courts in China. Mr. Williams, our able Secretary of Legation, speaking from an experience of twelve years, states that he is quite satisfied with their results. He says: " If the rules of procedure in Consular Courts are laid down with clearness, they can be followed by any person with a fair education, and the value of his decision can be increased by requiring him to get the advice of Assessors. Most of the cases in China consist ot damages for injury to persons or property, for debts or division of estates, such as require no high legal attainments for their equitable settlement " (1). I am aware that Mr. G. F. Seward had cases of the gravest character to try; but that was after he first came to China. Now the state of disorganization which prevailed in that country after the Franco-British war, and which was consequent partly on the opening of New Ports, andpartly on the existence of an insurrection, has passed away and the conclusions arrived at by Dr. Williams may be looked upon, perfectly reliable.

Supervisory powers of Inspectors of Consulates and of Consuls-General over Consuls.

Neither would the establishment of a Court of appeal in Shanghai prove of any benefit in connection with the superior. powers which it would confer upon the Consul-General. This officer has enough to do with his owns Consulate without being burdened with the care of affairs at the other Ports, unless a Consul be appointed, besides the Consul-General, for Shanghai ; and this would be, I think, a most useless expense. Moreover the great distance of Shanghai from the various Ports ; the delays in receiving and transmitting communications between it and the minor Ports, the peculiar aspect which every case assumes according to the circumstances of places, render it necessary to leave much to the discretion and good judgment of the local officers at points so far apart in this vast Empire; and, if a Consul is capable and devoted ; if he has due regard to standing instructions, no one better than himself can protect the interests of his country in his District. To all illuse of power or errors of judgment by the Consuls, the Inspector of Consulates, who would always intervene on the spot, would prove an effective check without embarrassing their action, a thing which the Consul General

---

(1) Mr. Williams to Baron Rehfues – Peking, June 26, 1868. Diplomatic correspondence,—1868,—Part 1; page 562.

might, however unwillingly, do if he were allowed to use, at a distance, the powers which I propose to delegate to an Inspector.

I now come to the details of the grouping of the various Consulates. Tientsin being the most important of the three northern Ports and only eighty seven miles South west of Pau-Ting-fu, the capital of the Province of Che-li, where the Governor General of Che-li, and Shan-tung resides, would be the seat of a Consul who would have two Agents under him, one at New-chwang, in the territory of Sing-king, also called Liu-tung, and the other at Che-foo, in the Province of Shang-tung.

<small>The grouping of Cosul-ates, the Tient-sin group.</small>

Shanghai would be the natural centre for the Ports of Chin-kiang and Ningpo, not because of its political importance, but on occount of its being,. as our able Consul General, Mr. Seward names it, the great commercial port of the Asiatic Coast and the place where more Americans congregate than at all the other points in China.—Ningpo being in the Che-kiang, would be made a dependency of the Foochow Consulate were it not that all its steam communications are with Shanghai. Chin-kiang is a very important port owing to its proportion of inland trade which at present is greater than at any other Port in the Empire, and on that account, it would require an officer of the first order, whose jurisdiction would extend over Wu-hu if it should be opened.

<small>The Shanghai group.</small>

Hankow being situated opposite Woo-chang foo (武昌), which is the residence of the Governor General of Hoo-kuang, (湖廣) or the Two Hoo, as it is generally called, and which comprise the Province North of the Lake, Hoo-pei, and the province South of the Lake, Hoonan, and being frequented by many American steamers, it should be the station of a Consul of great experience, who would have jurisdiction over Kiukiang (九江) in the province at Kiangsi and any ports that may hereafter be opened further to the Westward on the Yang-tsze, Yu-chow (岳州) and Sha-she (沙市) where he would have agents who would transact all business of importance through him. Yu Chow is the key to the Province of Hoonan and lies at the entrance of the Tung-ting Lake (洞庭湖) which is the Great thoroughfare of Hoonan, rich in timber of all sorts, Coal, Tea and rice. Sha she is the Great entrepôt for the trade of the province of Sze Chuen; all the light draught boats which are built to navigate the rapids of the Yang-tsze, which terminate

<small>The Hankow group.</small>

about forty miles above Yih-chang (宜 昌), tranship their cargoes into large vessels that convey them down the Great River Yang-tsze, which discharges itself in to the sea near Shanghai.

The Foochow group. Foochow-foo the place of residence of the Governor General of Fookien and Chekiang, the Tea Districts, Pagoda Anchorage, where the Chinese have an immense Arsenal and a Dock Yard, built on foreign style by officers of the French Navy, Wanchu, to the Northern, if it should be opened, would be placed under one Consul residing at Foochow-foo with agents under him.

The Amoy group. Amoy, the door to the Fookien Province, as its name in Chinese indicates, would be the proper residence for a Consul whose jurisdiction would extend over agents at Swatow and Vice-Consuls for the Formosa ports.

The Canton group. Wampoa and the Island of Hainan would come under the Consul residing at Kwang-chiu-Fu, or Canton, as it is called by foreigners, it being the seat of office of the Governor General of Kwang-Tung and Kwang-se. Canton is a Port of much importance; the proportion of the American Trade being probably greater there than at any other Port except Shanghai.

The Term of Office for which Consuls should be appointed. I have now to refer to the term of office for which Consuls in China should be appointed. Doubtless the practice of removing an officer without just cause is injurious to the service and should be abolished. Yet I would not advocate life appointments with pension at the end of a term of years, they being, I believe, too often productive of indifference to public interest and apt to close the door to worthy men. In the Consular service in China, like in the Army and the Navy, men with special knowledge and experience are required and, without giving life commissions to officers called to any office in the East, I should suggest the enactment of a law by which persons sent there could not be removed at the end of a Presidential term unless they have failed to fill their post to their credit and to that of their own Country; and therefore the reasons given for their removal should be flagrant.

The Interpreter Corps. I would propose to give still greater guarantees to the officers of the Interpreter Corps from which the Vice-Consuls, Consulars Agents and Consular Clerks would be recruited. Such men should receive permanent appointments with pension after thirty years service. Of necessity Student Interpreters come to China when yet very young, and before they have received the after school training which, in America, opens the door to almost every career; and, so arduous is their task, that, after they have acquired a sufficient knowledge of the language, their early years have gone by and they are only fitted for the special and arduous duties to which the most competent are known to have devoted a life-time. I should suggest the appointment of six Interpreters with a Salary of $2,500 for Tientsin, Shanghai, Hankow, Foochow, Amoy and Canton, and of ten Student Interpreters, with a Salary of $1,800, to be distributed among the minor ports, such as New-chwang, Che-foo, Chin-kiang, Ningpo, Kiu-kiang, Wuhu, Wanchu Tamsui, Taiwan-foo and Hainan, where they would officiate as Consular Agents or Vice-Consuls. It has been proposed by Mr. Seward, our able Consul General, to appoint three or four interpreters to reside at Ports known to be the rendez-vous of a large number of American vessels but where, as a general thing, Consuls hold little or no intercourse with native officials, owing to the fact that there are, in the District, no American interests to protect, except such as are connected with the entering and clearing of vessels, the shipping of cargo, all of which is transacted through foreign Commissioners of Customs in the employ of the Chinese. At other points, like Foochow-foo, Amoy, Tamsuy, and the ports of Formosa, where our shipping is inconsiderable, but where the inland traffic in articles of export to the United States, although not as great as it is in Shanghai, Canton &c., is still of much importance, and therefore where Consuls and Native Officials have daily opportunities to discuss the perplexing questions connected with the Inland trade, it is proposed to suppress the office of Interpreter and to make simple allowance for their occasional services. If this were done, doubtless the consular prestige, at points much visited by our vessels, will gain with scarcely other benefit to us than the satisfaction of our national pride, while the development of our internal relations with China will be sacrificed at places which, owing to the peculiar production of the soil, must soon become great centers of exchange of trade between the Pacific States and China.

Services which Interpreters can render.

If I were to undertake the task of securing durable concessions from the Chinese and had to select for assistance between a whole squadron, and an able interpreter, although I concede that Diplomacy, not assisted by force, will never accomplish anything of any consequence in the East, I would rather incline for the latter. In two of the most important cases I ever had with the Chinese during my term of five years, I was indebted for success to the friends who aided me in communicating with the Chinese, Dr. Talmage, who so often has revised translations of my dispatches and Baron de Meritens, of Foochow, who more than once has presented them to the Vice-Roy of Fookien and Chekiang and commented on them to him to render their affect more decisive. In the case of the Rover, where the influence of the Ministers, the demonstration of force by admiral Bell had failed, words of persuasion, properly offered, made the Chinese do what the most sanguine had never expected to obtain from them even with the assistance of what they call the moral influence of our fleet. In the case of the Amoy Dock, which had been in Peking for eight years before I took hold of it, without the aid of the Minister, in three months, through the Vice-Roy of Chekiang and Fookien, I gained my point. It was said at the time that I had used force. I need not say that I had not, and I can refer those who would remain incredulous, to my correspondence. And if I quote these cases, it is because they are well known in southern China, their happy termination having been the source of general benefit, and by these examples I may demonstrate more conclusively what we can accomplish with good Interpreters and how important it is to give to the organization of a Corps of those officers the attention it deserves.

The Salary of Consular officers.

In coming to the pecuniary considerations of this subject, I shall be extremely brief, having already extended over it in a previous despatch to the Minister, copy of which was sent to the Department. Suffice it to say, therefore, that, under the present regime, an officer, with ordinary family obligations, is unable to sustain the drain forced upon his limited resources by the requirements of his official position, and which are not supplied by the country, and, therefore, one of the two, either he must see the service suffer or resign a post the responsibilities of which he has accepted and which he finds he is unable to properly sustain. And yet, to answer the requirements of every Consulate, but a very small proportion of the income which the United States derive from the China trade need be expended. As regards the Amoy District, constituted as it is a little more than one per cent (or $16,180) of the annual revenue accruing to the country from the export trade of the five ports therein, would supply all its demands. As it is not generally known that this income is so large, I will offer a few figures showing its importance. From Amoy 5,453,370 lbs. of Tea were sent to the United States during the seasons 1868-69, on which were paid to the Treasury a duty of $1,363,342 Gold coin. In 1869 not less than 741,589 lbs. of Tea were shipped from Tamsui to our markets, and besides 450,000 lbs. of Camphor, direct from the same Port to New York, the duties on Tea alone amounting to over $178,000 Gold coin. Southern Formosa does not count yet for anything in the exports to America. But doubtless, before long, Camphor, Tea and Sugar will form an important items of trade between that region and the United States. A trial shipment of Sugar to California, through Japan, was made from Takao, in Southern Formosa, at the end of 1870.

Coolie Trade. I should have desired not to close this series of memoranda without alluding to the coolie trade; but besides that the notes which I have given you on the additional legislation which, I believe, is required, to make the laws of 1862 thoroughly effective, and the voluminous correspondence which I have transmitted to the Department in 1867 and 1869, doubtless, will afford you sufficient information on this most important subject, the great length of this paper prevents me from further extending over it, and I will beg privilege to offer a few concluding remarks.

Amoy, 20th April 1871.

CONCLUSIONS.

CONCLUSIONS.

> In peaceful and tranquil times, be strictly just. When the people are obstinate and unyielding, rule them by severity; when they are harmonious and compliant, govern them with mildness; when they are deeply sunk in barbarity, rule them with rigor.
> (The Shoo-king, Book of Show section VI).

If the premises given in the foregoing paper are correct, the following deductions are equally true. Unless directly or indirectly, through our guns or through the Inspector General who, of late, has virtually become an irresponsible Secretary of Foreign Affairs to the Chinese, we are prepared to absorb China and substitute in a day (trade would not stand the delays and constant changes which must be the result of a regular crusade) over those 360,000,000 of people, our system of Government, and the mechanism of our administration of public affairs, we have either to give up all idea of ever giving effect to the terms of the treaties, or to devise means of carring them out which will prove satisfactory to the Chinese. I do not suppose that there is any foreign power, in our days, except Russia, that seriously thinks of conquering China. In my opinion there is no doubt that she has such a desire, although I could not give any proof. "One can only judge by analogy. They have extended themselves in Asia wherever they have had the opportunity and they have recently conquered and annexed the kingdom of Bokkara at great cost, completing the extension of their dominions in that quarter to the borders of British India, a boundary which they must accept as final in that direction. The difficulties in that enterprise were greater, and the advantages not to be mentioned as compared to those to be incurred or gained in the acquisition of China. In the actual direction of this Empire, they have taken and occupied with forts within a few years, the great tract of country lying between the Amoor and the present frontier, without any advantage in the region itself to attract them, and apparently only for the object of reaching nearer to China proper. They obtained a valuable fort upon the coast, but that they could have had without the costly annexation of so great a territory."

"They have more young men learning the Chinese language in one way or another than all the other Westerns together, and they push their traders into the country with a pertinacity quite uncalled for by the exigencies of heir trade.

"Finally, there lie₃ before them a prize unsurpassed in the history of the World! A nation of at least 200 millions of industrious, energetic and ingenious people, ripe for conquest, and capable, when conquered, of giving inexhaustible supplies of excellent soldiers and sailors; a nation poor indeed in resources at present, but capable of a miraculous resurrection under an energetic rule. A country full of natural wealth, with an area of fertile soil already under cultivation; with a system of navigable rivers unsurpassed in the world; a coast abounding in fine harbours and commanding this side of the Pacific; a dominion extending to the tropics and including in its wide embrace every climate and almost every valuable production of the earth."

"It is impossible that, with their antecedents, their settled policy for centuries, the Russian should fail in desire for such a prize as this. As for the power, unless succoured by other Western nations, the country would lies defenceless before the assault of 50,000 men led by a General skilled in modern war. Such succour, if it came at all, would probably come too late. By occupying the western and north western Provinces under one pretext or an other, and with the declaration that it was provisional or temporary, they could fairly reach the coast and have possession of the main strategical points with two or three hundred thousand Chinese soldiers under arms and in effective condition, before any European power, could have concluded to intervene. Their conclusions then would be uninteresting." (1)

In view of this greatest of hazards, a man who has had a great experience of China was writing in 1864. "When a strong and highly civilized nation comes in contact with one weaker and lower in the scale of civilization, one of two things, I fancy, must happen,—either the inferior must be raised by a process to the level of the more civilized power, or it will not be raised. In which case it must sooner or later succumb to the stronger by whom it will be conquered. China must be regenerated, or remain stationary, and be parcelled out among foreign powers; and our present policy is fast tending towards that end." (2)

---

(1) A letter from Mr. Edward Cunningham, an American Citizen, residing in Shanghai, to Mr. George F. Seward, U. S. Consul-General in China, 1869.
(2) Our interests in China &c. by Ho.atio N. Lay, C. B., late Inspector General of Chinese Customs.

Mr. Hart who has been under Mr. Lay was fully satisfied with the correctness of these views and his aim has been to save China from herself by inducing her to substitute western civilization for her own. But, to accomplish this, a revolution was required by which the rule of the Literati must come to an end; and that was simply an impossible undertaking. Ché-Hwang-té (B. C. 220) before Mr. Hart, had conceived the same plan; and, to make sure of it, in eastern style, he had ordered the burial alive of those of the Literati who would oppose his rule, and the burning of their books, that no trace would ever remain of them in the Empire. This was carried out to the letter. Yet, when twenty two years later, his successor, Vanti, of the Kan Dynasty, undertook to revive literature, he found little or no obstacle. The books had disappeared, it is true, but their contents having been committed to memory by old men, and by them to their children, they soon came again to light. Since then the Literati have been submitted to many persecutions, but their power has survived them all, and, to-day, they reign as supreme over China as they did two thousand years ago. The Tartars have conquered China, they have issued death warrants against them, they have revived the laws of Ché-Hwang-té against their books; but both have resisted the trial, and the Tartars themselves have finally been absorbed by the civilization which many of their Emperors had made it their task to destroy.

It is easy to conceive what a fault Mr. Hart committed in disclosing his plans to the Literati who, in self defence, had to oppose him. And whatever he may do to amend his error, I fear, it is a fatal one, and that his scheme will never obtain the countenance of the rulers of China. As it is now, a statesman would have no other course to take but to openly condemn, from the start, what has been done for ten years past. Standing upon the platform of respect for treaties which, even with savages, is a platform, I should think he would require their fulfilment from the Chinese. Under that platform, it must be conceded by the Cabinet of Peking that direct relations, being the result of the expedition of 1860, the audience question must be settled. Having once gained access to the person of the Emperor, our Statesman should give him plainly to understand that war with the foreign powers means defeat to Chinese arms and therefore the fall of his Dynasty. And I believe that, sooner than have war, the Emperor who knows that China is not ready, would make many concessions. But if we wait two years longer, perhaps less, he will listen to nothing. Being better prepared, the Chinese will consider themselves invulnerable; they will take the aggressive and make an desperate attempt to expel us for ever from their country. And a most bloody war will be the result of our policy of peace.

I do not advocate the abuse of our position by making inconsiderate demands upon China. Rendered wise by the experience of Europe where, forty years ago, the same reforms which we now propose to China were introduced, we could save her the sad experience which one of her greatest statesman and the most honest of our opponents, Tseng-kou-fan so much apprehends for her, and which, indeed, must result from an inconsiderate and too rapid advance in the road to progress. But we should insist upon a beginning being made in the right direction by a fair inauguration of the inland trade which our Ministers could easily protect through the pacific means which I have recommended and through their moral influence at the capital and demonstration of force, at given points, whenever it should be judged necessary to resort to such extreme steps. But I am sure that, almost always, if the Ministers and the Consuls will be prompt and firm, such calamities as must result from a resort to force, could be avoided. Having thus shown the Chinese that we are as ready to go towards them as we are determined that they shall come to us, and the race, so to speak, between the two Civilizations being once fairly progressing, we could safely look for results from time.

Russia, in this, has shown us how to proceed. She has her frontier touching the Chinese frontier. Her treaties, it is true, contain very few provisions which can be construed as protective of the rights and the liberty of her subjects engaged in the China trade, but she has given the cabinet of Peking to understand that her merchants, how far they may go from their flags, are always under its protection and that they must not be molested, and it is well known at Peking that if they should ever molest a Russian, the coloring of the map of the North East of Asia would soon to have to undergo a material change. The appropriation by the Russians of the few provinces which they have "annexed" of late years teaches the Chinese a better lesson than to play off Yang-chow or Formosa tactics with the Czar or to levy 17½ per cent on brick tea instead of 2½. When we have said this, we have shown the Russian policy in China. When our Ministers either court the Chinese, or bully them, the Russian Ministers remain silent. They never talk, but they always act, and constantly in the same way. And that frightful regularity has an incredible effect on the chinese character. It has with these people something of the power of fate; and, strange to say, with all this, Russians are most popular with the Chinese. Native officers have aften told me that they consider them less troublesome than most foreigners.

It is true that, unlike Russia, we have no common frontier with China. But surely her coast is at our mercy, and we may lay our hands on that portion of her revenue which accrues from foreign trade, whenever we may choose to do so. Let the Cabinet of Peking once understand that a system of reprisal similar to that which the late Mr. Gibson attempted to inaugurate in Formosa, will be applied by our Consuls in every case when the lives and property of our citizens shall be in danger, and, in other cases of serious violation of our treaty rights, by the Ministers, and we will not have to record over again outrages like the Tientsin Massacre, or the farces connected with the interpretation which has been given, for the last ten years, to the 48th Article of the British Treaty of Tientsin.

I must not be understood to advocate a policy of blood and discord for which I have as much repugnance as the advocates of the "laisser faire" policy. But I hold that the *lex talionis* adapts better than any other to an Eastern race. It has been inaugurated by the greatest legislators from the plains of Arabia to the banks of the Yellow river, and surely we cannot disregard, without endangering the ultimate success of our mission in the East, the lessons taught to us by an experience of thousands of years:—and I am convinced that we commit a great fault in not applying it to China, whenever circumstances of undoubted gravity demonstrate that we should treat the natives or their Rulers with unusual rigour. It would be in vain that we should attempt making any impression upon them through any others means.

How severe this regime may seem, it would not exclude the milder form of dealing with man which are in use among Christian nations; and, in ordinary times, no opportunities should be lost by which the Chinese may be shown that we have, naturally, a high sense of equity and moderation. This may be done through the Interpreter-judges and the Inspectors and the special legislation which I have recommended in Memorandum No. 5. Indeed, this pure administration of Justice at the remotest parts of the Empire, could not fail to work incalculable good in undermining little by little and without shocks, but surely, the foundations upon which the social and political organization of the Chinese is based. Again, the unfortunate construction placed upon several articles of the treaties, being removed, I should not think that there would be many serious causes of opposition to the inland trade left to either the local or provincial authorities; and I believe that both would cease to resist a system sanctioned by their masters for the unobstructed working of which they might be easily made responsible. Nay, finding in the foreign activity sure means to increase trade, and, thereby, their income, they would soon favor the extension of its field. The facilities which they now give to Russian Merchants who have disdained availing themselves of any exterritorial rights, may be a hint of what they would do in our case, if we should conclude to interfere less imprudently and unnecessarily than we have done heretofore with the native officers, rights and privileges. The opening of the inland trade would not only contribute in serving the foreign interests in China; it would inaugurate a new era in the history of our relations with this people. Through it Foreigners and Natives, being placed in more frequent and closer contact, would learn how to appreciate their respective qualities and put up with each other's ways and manners. Soon mutual confidence would reign between the two races and the causes of dissension and conflict would gradually decrease. This would not be the result of one days' labor, but it would surely come in the end. A result which we shall never obtain if we persit in the policy of isolation and "laisser faire" which we have adopted during the last ten years.

It cannot be argued that the adoption of these views would be the beginning of a policy of interference which it has been the aim of the United States to avoid with every nation, since the Declaration of Independence, and, therefore resisted. For, has not a deviation from this traditional policy been already decided upon as regards China? Is not the fact of our citizens' presence on the sacred soil of the Empire under the terms of treaties which we know were not willingly signed by China, a most flagrant violation of this most solemn principle of non-interference? Is not that article of the Treaty as regards Christianity which, in condemning the worship of ancestors places itself in direct opposition to the fundamental law of the Empire, a most flagrant interference in the affairs of the Chinese? (1) This deviation from our traditional policy has been decided upon in the interest of Civilization, that China should not be longer tolerated to remain in her suicidal isolation from the balance of the world. What we have thought well to do in 1842 and 1858 in the interest of Religion and Civilization, we can surely do now to save a great nation from irreparable sufferings and perhaps ruin. If the first interference was justified by the motives which dictated it, the second shall be worthy of praise, and will gain to us not only the acclamations of the rest of the world but, in the long run, the gratitude of the Chinese nation,—and this is why I advocate it in such strong terms.

AMOY, 21st April 1871.

(1) See the Shoo-king. Part the V, the Books of Show, Book 1, The great declaration. Part L.

APPENDIX.

APPENDIX.

On page 119 of this paper, in connection with services which Interpreters can render, I say:—"If I were to undertake the task of securing durable concessions from the Chinese and had to select for assistance between a whole squadron, and an able interpreter, although I concede that Diplomacy, not assisted by force, will never accomplish anything of any consequence in the East, I would rather incline for the latter. In two of the most important cases I ever had with the Chinese during my term of five years, I was indebted for success to the friends who aided me in communicating with the Chinese, Dr. Talmage, who so often has revised translations of my dispatches and Baron de Meritens, of Foochow, who more than once has presented them to the Vice-Roy of Fookien and Chekiang and commented on them to him to render their affect more decisive."

As I might be misunderstood in the use I make of the word *persuasion*, I think it but just that I should, at least, give the words which I used in carrying out my points in one of the two cases which I quote, that of the *Rover*, inasmuch as the truth that I conveyed to the Chinese authorities, in the despatch alluded to, was much more terrible to them than the presence of a whole fleet. As regards the massacre of the crew of the American Barque *Rover*, on the southern end of the Island of Formosa, I only took the matter in hand and independently from any one else, after the disastrous visit of the U. S. flag-ship *Hartford* to the scene of the occurrence which resulted in the death of Lieutenant commander Mackenzie, who was killed in an encounter with the natives, and the immediate withdrawal of our forces. After Rear-Admiral Bell had declined to cooperate with me on the plea that he had no available forces, I wrote the Governor-General the despatche hereunder given and which I antedated that it might appear as having been written before the intelligence of the disaster met with by the Admiral had reached me. It is translated almost literally from the Chinese version.

The effect of this despatch was all that could be desired. The Vice-Roy ordered an expedition to proceed to the place where the *Rover's* crew had been murdered, and in order to enable me to accompany the expedition, he placed one of his own steamers at my disposal; and ninety days afterwards, and at the end of a campaign which lasted forty-five days, and during which the Chinese lost one eighth of their forces through hardship and disease, the desired satisfaction was obtained and the agreement entered into at the time, with the natives, for the protection of castaways has never since been broken. (See Diplomatic correspondence for 1867-1868—China—also commercial relations for 1869 and the Chinese Customs Gazette for December 1870).

U. S. CONSULATE, *Amoy* 22nd June 1867.

The sudden conclusion you have come to in the affair of the *Rover* and the reasons you give disappoint me extremely. You had never seemed to doubt, before this, that the Rover had been wrecked on the Chinese seas and that her crew had been murdered on Chinese Territory. If you ever had any doubt left on this point, why not say so and settle the question, at once, by a glance over the map, when called upon by Captain Febiger and by myself, on the 20th of April last, to lend your aid towards investigating this distressing affair? Then, and not now, was the time to present your objections. For then the monsoon was favorable to naval operations in the southern Bay of Formosa. Then the hot weather had not set in; then we had our forces near the spot. Then many of the unfortunate victims who, by this time, doubtless have perished through violence, exposure or starvation, were, I doubt not, living. The remains of those that had been murdered, since rendered irrecognisable by the action of time, or scattered to the winds, could have been recovered and sent to their friends for sepulture. All this we could have accomplished without other people's help and on our own responsibility, had we only known your designs; and we could have reserved our rights for, such indemnity, as we may have been justified to ask by your former inaction. But your language differed much from what it now is. You prayed us to do nothing and you promised that you would do everything that was asked. In fact you wrote me: "On receipt of information relative to the massacre of the master and crew of the Bark *Rover* by the savages, previous to your arrival, we have issued directions to the civil and military authorities to adopt measures for the management of this affair * * * and if any exertion of zeal can do it, no endeavours will be spared to bring the offenders to immediate punishment, in order that terms of good fellowship and harmony may exist between China and the foreign powers. We could not dare troubling Captain Febiger and yourself for military and naval assistance in the matter, since, in the event of any accident, we would feel more than ever grieved- We have again directed the civil and military authorities to despatch troops and constabulary to carry on operations." * * * (April 19th 1867). On the 20th, that is to say the day after this letter was written, we received the same assurance of your readiness to comply with our just request, and the General only required a few days to perfect his plans, his past experience of mountain warfare being limited. But he promised to act promptly and simply asked for liberty to strike the blow alone. He said to me: "If any force can bring these savages to terms the Chinese soldiers are adequate to the task; but being alone responsible to my Government for the success of the expedition it is but justice that I should conduct it with entire liberty of action and I decline accepting any assistance on the part of foreign nations." Under the circumstances Captain Febiger and myself determined to remain passive of observers, feeling that you thoroughly understood the extent of your obligations under the Treaty and that you had made up your mind to discharge them with celerity and honor. And we fully realized that, from that day, we could not take any step in advance of you, that would relieve your Government of all responsibility with the United States without interfering with the claims for indemnity which must be made on behalf of such of the survivors of the *Rover's* crew as it was expected would be saved through your exertions, should you fail to fulfill your obligations. * * * You cannot claim that, at the time, you ignored the name of the locality where the *Rover* had met her fate, for you furnished it to me in your despatch of the 19th April and said it is, "Red head Island." Neither did you ignore that of the bay where the *Rover's* crew were murdered, for, in the same despatch, you informed me it is called Ku-wa-shu-pi-suan, by the natives. Later you notified me that your officers were only waiting for your final orders, their first column being ready to advance and that they would soon prove by their acts that the Chinese Government entertained the most kind feelings for the Western nations.

How different your language now! Those same officers, Tin-Pau. Chew-Chang and Pen-key who yesterday were about to accomplish so much, having examined the Treaty, suddenly find out that they can do nothing. According to your own statement, they report: "Art. 11 and 13 provide that whenever, within the jurisdiction of the Emperor of China, either on shore or at sea, any one who shall molest Americans, shall be punished by the civil and military authorities to the best of their ability, But as in the *Rover's* case, the Americans were not murdered in Chinese territory, or on Chinese seas, but on a region occupied by savage tribes, relief cannot be asked for under the treaty. Were it in our power to seize the murderers, we would gladly do so, that the Chinese might keep friendly intercourse with foreigners. But the savage region does not come within the limits of our jurisdiction &c. &c." As for yourself, far from disavowing such words so different from your own, you state that, "Your impression is that your subordinates have furnished you with a true statement of the case and you believe that those savages are wild animals with whom any one would disdain to contend."

Such being the conclusions you have arrived at, I will remark that this correspondence has now lasted longer than it should, and that it has to be brought to a close by a fair understanding on both parts of what our respective rights and duties are. In consequence I beg to reaffirm what I have said, or written to you at former times, that the United States, in this case as in any other, will insist upon a strict observance of the treaties. And I may remark that, on the 3rd moon, 15th day, 6th year, appearing to fully understand Capt. Febiger and myself, you promised to afford prompt relief to the *Rover's* crew, to punish the murderers of our countrymen, that two months have elapsed since and that nothing has been done on you part towards keeping this most sacred engagement, having only discovered at this late hour, through your agents, that you are not expected under the Treaty, to keep your promises, in as much as they were made in ignorance of certain facts which have since been made known to you.

I am sure the Government of the United States will not accept such an issue, and, in its name, I protest emphatically, pardon me the expression, against this shifting way of dealing in this most important case, and I make all possible reserves for all claims in indemnity and reparation which may hereafter be brought forward in consequence thereof, by my Government against yours.

However it may be well for you to consider that the question involved in the wreck of the *Rover* and the murder of her crew by the natives of southern Formosa, a dependency of the Chinese Empire, does not only affect the American interests but also the interests of every one of the western powers that are connected by trade with China and whose ships ply between the Spanish, Dutch and English possessions, South, South East, and South West from Formosa, the various ports of China, on the Coast south of Amoy and those on the North of it. These vessels, either following their natural or direct route, or carried out of it by the winds, are apt to come to grief on or near the breakers on which the *Rover* was lost, and, of necessity, must seek for refuge in the bay at the South of Formosa Island. For if they go to the eastern of it, they find an abrupt coast where even an ordinary embarcation would not be safe, and if they go farther to the north on the Western coast, they must not stop until they reach Liang-Kiaw Bay which is, at least 15 miles distant. Can they afford always this long run? The deposition of the last known survivor of the *Rover's* crew, seems to show that this is not always practicable. They made the attempt and they had to stop, having soon become exhausted by fatigue, thirst and hunger. So that nine times out of ten they must stop in the Southern Bay which appears to have been opened by the Almighty as a natural refuge against the uncertainty of the elements. Hence humanity makes it a law to civilized nations to see that that portion of Formosa is kept clear of any of the inhospitable hordes that infest it, and if your Government does not do it, on the ground that it has no jurisdiction therein, or, that it has not the ability or the power to perform the task, the foreign powers will have to take the case in hand.

The United States would hear with regret that the Western nations have come to such expedient. For they have no desire to acquire any portion of the territory that must be occupied if it is resorted to; and the step, when taken, would be the first in the direction of a policy of violence that might ultimately end in the dismemberment of the Chinese Empire or at least its humiliation based on the incompetency of its authorities to command the respect of its own subjects or to fulfil certain obligations imposed by the laws of nations. I can assure you that it is the interest of the United States that you should be prosperous and powerful, and at peace with foreign nations and among your own people; and we have no ambitions designs to accomplish in regard to you, no desire to acquire any of your territory, having one already too large of our own; and the greater and more rich you become, the more mutually beneficial will be the trade between the two countries. Your prosperity will be for the good of the United States, and, whatever tends to impair it, a loss. Yet and with all this the United States form a great commercial nation and they are such above all. They desire the extension of trade all over the world and would not certainly sacrifice their interest to a blind friendship for China or any other country. And should any foreign power, being justified by the neglect or ill will of the Chinese, undertake the pacification by control of Southern Formosa, and clear it from the hordes that infest it, we would express no regret. The Southern end of the Formosa channel is a most important commercial thoroughfare which must be kept opened and free at all hazards. Having thus given you these assurances, it remains for me to show that, under the existing Laws of nations, the portion of Formosa settled by what you called the "*uncooked foreigners,*" or Savages, is one over which the western nations are justified in looking to the Government of China for the maintainance of order.

The Formosa tribes stands on the same footing with the Indians that inhabit yet a great portion of the United States. What I may say of one can apply to the other. As regard ourselves, for the sake of our interest, we have insisted with foreign nations that our Indians hold their existence as tribes at our exclusive will. Even if you never expected to interfere with the natives of Formosa further than to keep out the Agents of the foreign powers that might seduce them into foreign alliances, the result of which would probably be the absorption of the Island by a foreign ally, you should imitate us in our policy with these uncivilized people. For if you admit that such a territory has never been explored, you admit also that it can be seized by the first power that will find its interest to occupy it in advance of you, and that power shall acquire an indisputable right to its possession as the Spanish did when they discovered the New World, or as you did yourselves when you first implanted your colonies on the western shore of the Island. So you perceive the view we take of the native tribes of Formosa is that they should not be treated as independent, nor regarded as the owners of the soil they respectively live on; but that China has a right to that same soil because it occupies it at leisure. In fact this doctrine seem to to have been adopted by your Government, since the western Chinese farmers, when they find themselves crowded in their settlements keep advancing towards the Eastern Coast, the sword in their hands chasing the natives before them. And it is likely that they will do so until they have absorbed the whole country from the Formosa channel to the Pacific shore. And, in this, they only confirm, de facto, the rightness of the law I have quoted above and in virtue of which superior races, since the origin of the world, have, by degrees, substituted their civilization for that of an inferior one. The Chinese divide and parcel over the land of the natives of Formosa and grant it to their subjects as they need it, exactly as if it had been vacant and unoccupied land. They do more, anticipating the occupation of the native territory by their subjects, they controle in some instances, by the most arbitrary rules, the trade of the natives with the merchants of the western shores. The camphor, one of the most important staples of the Island, comes from the native mountains. No foreigner is allowed to export it or to acquire it therein. One single individual enjoys the exclusive right to carry on that traffic for the benefit of the Chinese Government; any one interfering with the right of the monopolist is put to death.

So the Chinese Government has even gone further with the natives of Formosa than the United States have gone with their Indians and, de facto, in the most flagrant manner, they have insisted for the last two hundred years upon a supreme power and dominion within the territory therein. This being the case, it is too firmly and clearly established to admit of dispute that the Formosa tribes are subject to the authority of China, and, although the country occupied by the natives is not within the limits of the various Chinese magistrates, the task of punishing any offence committed therein, whether the guilty party is a Chinese or a native, devolves on China and not upon the foreign powers. For if the native territory is not Chinese in population, it is Chinese in law and in fact, the Chinese Government having a sort of preemptive claim on it which it enforces every day through its subjects when it considers fit and advisable. * * * Sincerely hoping that this communication will tend to reform your judgment on many points of vital importance both to China and the United States, I give you the new expression of my high regards and esteem.

www.ingramcontent.com/pod-product-compliance
Lightning Source LLC
Chambersburg PA
CBHW030332170426
43202CB00010B/1095